CONNECTING
WOMEN

CONNECTING
WOMEN

A RELATIONAL GUIDE
for LEADERS *in*
WOMEN'S MINISTRY

LINDA
LESNIEWSKI

BakerBooks
Grand Rapids, Michigan

Published by Baker Books
a division of Baker Publishing Group
P.O. Box 6287, Grand Rapids, MI 49516-6287
www.bakerbooks.com

Printed in the United States of America

Library of Congress Cataloging-in-Publication Data
Lesniewski, Linda, 1949–
    Connecting women : a relational guide for leaders in women's ministry
/ Linda Lesniewski.
        p.   cm.
    Includes bibliographical references.
    ISBN 10: 0-8010-6811-8 (pbk.)
    ISBN 978-0-8010-6811-9 (pbk.)
    1. Women in church work. 2. Christian leadership. I. Title.
BV4415.L47 2007
253.082—dc22   2007026744

To Anne Murchison,
who lives her life
"in step" with the Holy Spirit.

CONTENTS

Acknowledgments   9
Introduction   11

Part I: Sharing God's Vision for Women
1. Sisterhood: Those Who Came Before   15
2. Hearing God's Voice   25
3. Making the Choice   35
4. Me, a Leader?   45

Part II: Heading Forward in Faith
5. Launching or Expanding a Ministry   61
6. Sharing the Vision   69
7. Talking So Men Will Understand   75
8. Partnering with Church Leadership   81
9. Connecting through Women's Ministry   93
10. Reaching Inward through Meeting Needs   103

Part III: Enjoying Fruitful Leadership
11. Nurturing Spiritual Growth   125
12. Sustaining Freshness: For Yourself and Your
      Ministry   137

13. Leading Leaders   151
14. Developing Generational Leaders   161

Part IV: Proclaiming His Message

15. Reaching Outward through Meeting Needs   175
16. Sharing Your Faith   183
17. Equipping and Sending   195
18. Contagious Devotion   205

Appendix 1: Understanding a Saving Relationship
    with Christ   213
Appendix 2: Leadership Team Member
    Guidelines   215
Appendix 3: Why Have a Women's Enrichment
    Ministry?   217
Appendix 4: Women's Ministry Survey   219
Appendix 5: Life Experiences Inventory   221
Appendix 6: Leading through the Power of the
    Holy Spirit   225
Appendix 7: Spiritual Gifts   227
Appendix 8: Mentoring   231
Appendix 9: Personal Leadership Prayers   237
Appendix 10: Sample Women's Ministries Mission
    Statements   241
Appendix 11: Ministry in Motion   243
Notes   245
Bibliography   253

ACKNOWLEDGMENTS

E very woman I've ever met has influenced my life, from
Mrs. Bolton, my first grade schoolteacher, to Vicki Neill,
my principal during the years I taught at Gary Elementary School. Almost daily I've met women who inspire me
with their faithfulness or courage. Writing about women was
easy because I've had an endless supply of stories!

My two daughters, Lori and Lisa, as well as my two daughters-in-love, Ashley and Erin, have provided a picture window into their generation. They've taught me by the ways
they prayerfully respond to the messages and challenges of
their world. My two sisters, Claudia and Nancy, as well as
my amazing sister-in-love, Jo Beth, model the importance
of healthy family relationships, for it's within family that
we learn and practice those relationship skills we bring to
the family of Christ.

My sisters-in-Christ who have lived these stories hold a
special place in my heart, for our lives intertwined to form
the chapters. We've planned, prayed, wept, and worshiped
together. Those women who meet monthly to offer their
wisdom and direction through our leadership team—Nancy
Paul, Donna Shay, Pam Thedford, Jennifer Paul, Cindy Dykes,
Sharon Schwartz, Shannon Smith, Jill Hardin, Noelle Courson,
and Mary Ann Lackland—are true comrades and soul mates.
The Encouraging.com writers influence me by their own commitment to ministry through the written word. Interns Amy
Packer and Rachel Bitter have impacted me with their re-

sponse to God's call to equip women in their generation for Christ. Peggy Tollett has prayed for me since I was in junior high school and continues to serve as a spiritual mentor.

Karen DeLeon has spent her life serving Christ internationally. Her courageous heart has emboldened mine. The use of her secluded stateside cabin provided the tranquility for turning random notes into paragraphs and chapters. Ruth Tamez and Celia Sanchez have introduced me into the culture of the Hispanic woman, and Rasha Sara has sensitized me to the realities of the Christian Arabic-speaking woman. The comradeship of Chris Adams and the LifeWay Ministry Multipliers has challenged me to new levels of commitment and has comforted me when I struggled.

Cindy, whom I dare not identify as "my pastor's wife," has modeled authenticity and strength of character to stand against the pressures of conformity. Lynda Speak's dedication and servant's heart joined hands as she proofed the manuscript. Vicki Crumpton, skilled editor and mentor, has gently encouraged me to new levels of learning. Then there's Mavita Markle who defies description. She's my trench mate and soul mate in both friendship and ministry. Her administrative assistance is a calling from God, and she serves with her "whole" heart. Thank you, sweet friend!

I can't leave out my husband, Gary, or my supervisor, Ken Warren, just because they're not women! Gary's constant encouragement and personal sacrifice helped me carve out time to write. His spiritual insights provided rich fodder when I "ran dry." Ken's gifted leadership and vision for women's ministry has fanned the flames of what God is doing among women at home and in churches everywhere. Thank you both for your key role in building the kingdom through ministry to and ministry through women.

WOMEN IN MOTION
*"Since we live by the Spirit
let us keep in step with the Spirit."*
Galatians 5:25

INTRODUCTION

Joyful tears flowed freely down Amber's cheeks as she asked Christ to be her Savior. Those tears contrasted with her sobbing as she relived the day Child Protective Services drove away with Madison, her twenty-one-month-old daughter. Amber had successfully completed rehab for prescription drug abuse and now struggled to find independent housing, a car, and a steady job—all criteria for getting her daughter back. She'd lost her father to drug abuse by age thirteen and her mother by age fifteen. By nineteen she was a single mom. She felt alone and hopeless.

Today Amber celebrates seven months of sobriety and five months of employment at a small flower shop. She rents an 850-square-foot fixer-upper completely furnished and scrubbed clean. She radiates the joy of a new believer and is investigating getting her GED and job training at a local junior college. Amber attends the "Single Mom Connection"[1] and Celebrate Recovery,[2] which provide supportive networks as she faces a hope-filled future one day at a time. Best of all, little Madison is back home and enjoying her mother's care.

What made the difference in Amber's feelings of hopelessness? Women networking through a local church made the difference. A lot happened during the two weeks that preceded Child Protective Service's home visit evaluating Amber's living situation. Sylvia located housing, assisted with contract negotiation, and organized the move. Bobbie collected furniture and helped with getting utilities turned on. She also arranged for medical assistance through a faith-based clinic. Dianne sewed curtains for the bedroom while Amber sorted through boxes and bags of donated clothing. Connie and Kathy caulked and cleaned in the bathroom and kitchen while their husbands mowed, trimmed, and hauled off debris. The day the housing passed inspection and Madison came home was one great day of celebration!

How did this network of women come into existence? Through the dreams, prayers, and actions of three women in a local church who stepped out in faith many years ago. That's what this book is about—developing leaders for networking women for discipleship and ministry within the local church. Each chapter begins with a real-life vignette of one woman's story. Through their stories, you'll catch glimpses of the changing face of women's ministry as God guides them to respond to the culture of their generation. The information that follows provides encouragement for those exploring these same areas of women's ministry. You'll begin to discover the process of God calling and equipping women in this generation. You'll join the excitement generated when God begins to work among and through women in the twenty-first-century church. Open your own heart to serving Christ, and just watch what happens in and around you as the Holy Spirit sets his great plan in motion for reaching women in this generation!

SHARING GOD'S VISION
FOR WOMEN

The journey of reaching women with God's love draws us together in an amazing adventure. We join with women who have sought one another's company from the earliest days as they worshiped and learned together. Part I will help you clarify God's call on your life as you sense the Holy Spirit moving you further along in your journey of faith. Some women are just beginning this journey, while others are seasoned veterans. Some women serve in small churches where they may sense God's call to begin a ministry to women. Others minister in larger churches with opportunities to expand programs and build teams of leaders. Wherever we are in the journey, we stand together in a sisterhood of believers that stretches back in time and forward into the future.

1

SISTERHOOD:
THOSE WHO CAME BEFORE

Teach me your ways so I may know you.
Exodus 33:13

Mothering twin girls required enormous energy and resourcefulness. Long days and isolation from other women produced a longing for friendships. Her church seemed the logical place to look. Soon a thriving Bible study group of women provided just the spiritual nourishment, prayer support, and interaction she sought. Chris's awareness of the needs of other women in the church grew from this earliest contact with the dynamics of women nurturing women. She wondered how this network of women could expand throughout the church to reach other women. Chris began praying and seeking to know God's plan for expressing his love to the women of her church. Little did she dream what God could do with her seeking heart.

How can God use me to reach out with Christ's love to challenge and to equip the women in my church?" I remember when that question first stirred in my heart.

If God has put these same longings in your heart, you stand in a long line of sisters bound by a common call.

All through God's Word, we see women seeking out other women for friendships and for spiritual nurturing. Ruth asked to remain with Naomi, her mother-in-law, after the death of her husband. Mary, the soon-to-be-mother of the Messiah, sought time with her pregnant cousin, Elizabeth. Dorcas so lovingly cared for her widowed friends that they sent for Peter when she died. Lydia regularly gathered with her women friends at the river to worship God. Joanna, Mary Magdalene, Suzanna, Mary the wife of Clopas, and Salome, along with Mary the mother of Jesus, traveled together and ministered to Christ and the disciples. They also stood with one another during the six long hours of Christ's crucifixion.

Was this pattern of women seeking out the company of other women in the heart of God as part of his design for the church? We see the emotion of loneliness in the earliest pages of Scripture even before the fall of man and woman. God said in Genesis 2:18, "It is not good for the man to be alone." In response, God created Eve for companionship for Adam. Sin shattered their idyllic world, though, and God sent them from the Garden of Eden into an unknown and frightening world. The new focus of their lives shifted from tending the garden to scratching a living from the soil and pain in childbirth.

Childbearing and related issues still consume a large portion of a woman's life. Science and medical technology have not eradicated PMS, infertility, miscarriages, untimely pregnancies, morning sickness, childbirth, postpartum depression, breast-feeding, diapers, and potty training. Who else but a woman could truly understand and encourage another woman in these areas? In Genesis, as well as in most of the Old Testament, we must read between the lines and study the culture to understand relationships among women. When we read the stories of the New Testament, though, we begin to see more clearly how women lived out these relationships.

Instruction to a Church Leader

One of the most popular passages in the New Testament concerning women's responsibilities to other women in the church comes from Paul's letter to Titus, a Gentile convert and church leader. Paul had previously left Titus on the island of Crete to help organize the work of the young church. In Titus 2:2–5, Paul instructed Titus what to teach the older men and women. Not surprisingly, his directives for women differed from the ones for the men. He told Titus to "teach the older men to be temperate, worthy of respect, self-controlled, and sound in faith, in love and in endurance." For the women, Paul included the responsibilities of teaching and training of younger women. Of course, the women also should be "reverent in the way they live, not to be slanderers or addicted to much wine." Those godly qualities certainly qualified them to teach and train others.

The teaching topics of the women in Titus's church parallel the same needs of the twenty-first-century woman. They still need to learn personal purity, parenting skills, strategies for building healthy homes, ways to minister to others, marriage skills, and conflict resolution. The end result then, as well as now, shows an unbelieving world the unique results of a life obedient and submissive to the Word of God.

A Lonely Woman

John 4:1–26 tells a story of a woman of mixed Jewish and Gentile heritage who encounters Christ at a well. Jesus, tired from his travels northward to Galilee and the relentless noontime sun, stops at the well to rest while the disciples head into town for food. We know from cultural observations that women typically drew water from the city well during the cool of the morning. They spiced the daily task with conversations and laughter with one another. For a woman to draw water at noon meant something was awry. Even though the law forbade a Jewish man to speak with a woman, especially a Samaritan woman, Jesus began a conversation by asking her for a drink of water. When he told her everything about her past, her five marriages, and a current live-in roommate, we realize the depth of her emotional isolation. We also assume she purposefully avoided the other women's judgmental attitudes by drawing water at a different time of day. After her conversation with Christ, she responded by hurrying into town seeking out anyone she could tell about this man, Jesus. The joy of meeting the merciful Messiah overcame her issues of shame.

Women today who feel those same pangs of separation and shame can rejoice with her when they see how Christ reached out to her with acceptance and a gift of living water! The same reaching out to those who struggle with a painful past can occur in today's church. Christian women only need sensitivity to the compassionate Christ who lives within them and who wants to invade a lonely heart.

Lydia and Worshiping Women

The book of Acts records the arrival of traveling companions Paul, Silas, Luke, and Timothy in Philippi of Macedonia, located across the bay from the eastern shores of modern-day Italy. On the Sabbath they went outside the city to locate a place of prayer, indicating that the city must have lacked the minimum quota of ten Jewish men to build a synagogue for worship. Paul and his companions discovered a group of women praying by the river and began speaking to them. Scripture says the Lord opened Lydia's heart to respond to Paul's message. Next Luke records that all of Lydia's family members were baptized as followers of Christ. In Acts 16:14–15, we see Lydia using her powers

19

of persuasion to have Paul and his companions come and stay at her house.

In this very same city, officials later flogged Paul and Silas, threw them into jail, and fastened their feet in stocks. You probably can recall the rest of this amazing story of hymns, earthquakes, loosened chains, and a jailer plus his whole household requesting baptism. What a great ending! Yet Luke adds one more bit of information. When Paul and Silas left the jail the next day, they headed straight to Lydia's house. Acts 16:40 records that they met with the brothers and encouraged them there.

One woman, drawn to worship with other women, ended up playing a significant role in Paul's missionary journey. She provided housing for Paul and his companions while they ministered in her city, as well as a welcoming place of respite after their release from prison. Wow! Luke was so blessed by this personal experience that he even chose to record it in his writings.

Dorcas and Her Widowed Friends

Widows have unique problems to confront in every century. Those in the culture during the time of Christ had even larger ones. Women who lost their husbands lost their sole source of income and provision. If they had no other family members to meet their needs, they looked to the church. In Acts 9:36–43, Luke records the story of Dorcas.[1] He describes her as a disciple "always doing good and helping the poor." Because Luke never mentions her husband, most assume she was also a widow. We first see the gathering of her widowed friends when she becomes ill and dies.

The leaders in Dorcas's church heard that Peter was in the nearby city of Lydda (about twelve miles away), so they sent two men to urge him to come right away. What a scene Peter witnesses as the mourning widows showed him all the robes and other clothing Dorcas had made. After sending everyone out of the room, Peter knelt and prayed, and then spoke to the dead woman: "Tabitha, get up." Dorcas opened her eyes, looked at Peter, and sat up. Just imagine the drama and excitement when Peter called everyone back into the room, and there stood Dorcas—alive! The news spread all over Joppa,[2] and as a result, many people believed in the Lord. One woman with a heart to do good ended up influencing an entire city for Christ, all because widowed friends and church leaders cared enough to seek out Peter's assistance on her behalf.

Godly Mothers, Grandmothers, Aunts, and Mothers-in-Law

We all long for a godly heritage. The Old Testament story of Ruth and her mother-in-law, Naomi, shows us the longing of a young woman to be influenced by a godly older woman. After her husband and father-in-law died, Ruth chose to leave her home and her people to travel with Naomi to an unknown land. That's how much Naomi's life and faith meant to Ruth. Her statement, "Where you go I will go, and where you stay I will stay. Your people will be my people and your God my God" (Ruth 1:16), has become a timeless declaration of true love frequently used at weddings. Few people realize it was a declaration of a daughter-in-law's devotion to a God-fearing mother-in-law.

In the first chapter of Luke, the announcement of the Messiah's coming by Gabriel to the young girl Mary ends with Mary heading to Elizabeth's house. Luke records that Elizabeth was in her sixth month of pregnancy when the angel Gabriel appeared to Mary, and that Mary remained with Elizabeth for about three months. During that time, these two women surely discussed the mystery of their pregnancies with one another. Perhaps Elizabeth nursed Mary

21

through her first trimester of nausea. Maybe Mary had the privilege of helping Elizabeth with the delivery. That personal childbirth experience would have been very helpful to Mary when she delivered her own child six months later in what we would consider less-than-desirable conditions (2:1–20).

We also see a tender story about godly heritage in Paul's second letter to Timothy. In chapter 1, Paul wrote how he longed to see Timothy and prayed for him day and night. He then reflected on Timothy's sincere faith, which first lived in his mother, Eunice, and his grandmother, Lois. Paul felt confident this same genuine faith now lived in Timothy. He acknowledged the spiritual investment Lois and Eunice made in Timothy's life, and God recorded it in his Word (vv. 3–5).

Today's more mobile culture creates additional issues. Even if God does bless a woman with a believing mother or grandmother, they probably live hundreds of miles away from her. They're not close by for wise counsel. In addition, divorce fragments homes. Dynamics become even more complicated when two fragmented families unite to form a new family. The church provides an excellent source for women to locate surrogate spiritual mothers and grandparents. The same spiritual mentoring Timothy received in AD 66 is available to women in the twenty-first-century church when Christian women assume the nurturing opportunities and responsibilities before them.

The Nurturing Environment of a Home

Priscilla modeled a different type of spiritual nurturing. Today we might call it discipling. She and her husband, Aquila, had opened their home to Christians for worship. We read in Acts 18:2–3 that they even housed Paul when he temporarily joined them in their tent-making business. This couple also invested their hearts and lives in Apollos, an important early church apologist. After arriving in Ephesus, Apollos "began to speak boldly in the synagogue [about Jesus]. When Priscilla and Aquila heard him, they invited him to their home and explained to him the way of God more adequately" (Acts 18:26). This same passage indicates Apollos knew the story of Jesus but only through his baptism by John the Baptist. Priscilla and Aquila shared the rest of the story with him at their house. Even though equipping and discipling can occur anywhere, the home offers an environment that frees ears to hear and hearts to respond.

Jesus also enjoyed the nurturing atmosphere of a home. He often stayed with Peter in Capernaum and in the home of three good friends—Lazarus, Mary, and Martha—when he visited Bethany, a small village located outside of Jerusalem. Just imagine the spiritual energy in a church today where women joyfully offer their home for ministry, for discipleship, for Bible study, and for nurturing servants like Apollos.

Coming Together for Ministry

I've loved studying the lives of women who had unique encounters with Jesus, then came together in ministry to him and his disciples.[3] Luke writes in Luke 8:2–3 about three specific women, "Mary (called Magdalene) from whom seven demons had come out; Joanna the wife of Cuza, the manager of Herod's household; Susanna. . . . These women were helping to support them out of their own means." Even though women might individually experience Christ's healing power and merciful grace in their lives, they often discover the strength of unity in serving him together. The church is part of God's design for expressing his grace and mercy to women through other women for each generation. We've seen it in the pages of Scripture during the earliest years of the church, and we see it today in the twenty-first-century church as women continue to gather for worship, for study, and for ministry.

23

For Reflection

1. What opportunities do the women in your church have for receiving guidance in the areas Titus mentions—parenting skills, personal purity, strategies for building healthy homes, ways to minister to others, marriage skills, and conflict resolution?

2. Christian women can reach out to those who struggle with a painful past. How do you see women's ministry reaching out in your church?

3. One woman, drawn to worship with other women, ended up playing a significant role in Paul's missionary journey. What do you and Lydia have in common?

4. The story of Ruth and her mother-in-law, Naomi, shows us the longing of a young woman to be influenced by a godly older woman. Who are some of the godly older women in your congregation?

2

HEARING GOD'S VOICE

The eyes of the LORD range throughout the earth to
strengthen those whose hearts are fully committed to him.

2 Chronicles 16:9

Kay enjoyed mothering her son and daughter, spending time with her husband, quilting, visiting with her twin sister, and being actively involved in her church. She had met for many months with several other women for Bible study and prayer, asking God to open the way for an active ministry to women in their church. As the small group looked for someone to provide leadership, her steady disposition and organizational abilities made her a likely candidate. In addition, each of the other women had personal responsibilities that prevented them from considering leadership. When the women expressed their desire for Kay to lead, she checked first with her husband, Tom, to make sure he was supportive. During the following days, she felt a variety of emotions. She eventually experienced freedom in her heart to accept the position, anxiety about such new responsibilities, and excitement about what lay in store for her and the women of the church.

God is the author and sustainer of a vibrant women's ministry, yet he uses individual women to implement what he creates. Perhaps you want to know if God is calling you into leadership. Perhaps you need to discern if he wants you to remain in leadership. Perhaps you are making decisions about the direction of a current ministry or feeling the need to restructure a particular facet of a ministry. The ability to find your way through any of these decisions becomes much clearer as you reflect on the status of your own relationship with God.

Discerning God's Call

My call came via the phone—literally! I'd taught a special education class in the local public schools for over five years when the phone rang one evening. The woman providing leadership for our women's ministry had accepted a new position, and the church had not found a replacement. She wondered if I would consider those responsibilities. I remember laughing! I responded with, "What? I'm a wife, a mother, and a special education teacher! I don't have any qualifications for that!" She gently pointed out two things: I was a Christian, and I was a woman. She then asked me to pray about it.

Pray, I did! My husband offered the same wise counsel he's offered many times before and since: "It never hurts to talk about it." So I did. I visited with some of the church staff and read over the job description. I then called my friend Joy for woman-to-woman counsel. She read the job description and announced, "Linda, this looks like a perfect match for your temperament, your life experiences, and your interests. I can really see you doing this."

That's all history now. I've experienced twelve years of the challenges and joys of leading women in ministry through my church. I have to admit that during the first year, I wondered if I'd made the right decision. I missed the daily hugs, waves, and smiles of my students as they called out, "Good morning, Mrs. Les!" I also stumbled through the challenges of computer competency and in-house church protocols. In addition, I had to transition from a campus of mainly female staff to an environment of mainly men. I quickly decided to move *learning the language of men* to the top of my must-do list!

Understanding how God speaks challenges all of us at some time or other in our spiritual journey, especially when we want to know if we're hearing him correctly. Examining the following areas of your spiritual walk can provide helpful insight in discerning God's will: your relationship with Christ, assurance of salvation, the role of the Holy Spirit, an attitude of obedience, a cleansed life, the study of God's Word, and ways to listen for God's voice.

A Personal Relationship with God

Knowing *about* God and his Son, Jesus, is distinctively different from knowing God *personally* through the work of his Son on the cross. It's a small difference in wording that makes a big difference in today, tomorrow, and eternity. My husband spent the first eighteen years of his life worshiping God. He had no doubts that Jesus was born as a baby to Mary and was crucified as a sacrifice for our sin. Yet this knowledge of God did not make a difference in his life. He still experienced an empty longing inside. After hearing three separate explanations of God's provision for his sin, Gary realized what he needed to do. Silently, he prayed, "Lord Jesus, I know I am a sinner. Please forgive my sins. Come into my life and be Lord of my life." That moment became a pivotal point in Gary's life. The empty longing inside disappeared, and a personal relationship with Christ began that continues to grow to this day, thirty-eight years later.[1]

As you continue this journey of discerning God's leadership and his will for your life in women's ministry, take time to reflect on your own relationship with God. Can you remember a time you spoke directly to God about his gift of salvation and your need for it? Do you have the assurance that you have established that eternal one-on-one saving relationship with God? If so, rejoice! Later we'll spend time discussing how you can summarize that experience so you can share it with others.

If you can't recall a time you talked to God about salvation and still feel that longing or emptiness inside, go to appendix 1 for more information to guide you in making that all-important decision.

Assurance of Salvation

Occasionally I visit with women who remember praying for salvation as a child, but they've never felt confident that a personal relationship with God existed as part of their life. Or perhaps they had this confidence for a while, but they drifted away and no longer feel the vibrant faith they once had. If you're in that first category of doubting the validity of your earlier experience, then I encourage you to take time to visit with God about it. Tell him of your concerns and your doubts. Ask him to clarify your relationship in your heart. Ask him to forgive your sins and become Lord of your life and bring with him the assurance that you belong to him for now and for eternity. Do it right now! He truly desires that you rest in his love and have confidence in your adoption into his forever family.

For those who have drifted away and no longer experience the joy a new life in Christ brings, there's great news. Jesus wants joy to be part of your relationship, and he's provided a way for you to have it. Joy is a natural result of the Holy Spirit's residence in your life.

The night before soldiers arrested Christ, he shared the Passover meal with his disciples. Afterward, the apostle John recorded a very special extended time of teaching. Christ taught on many topics that night, including the person of the Holy Spirit.

The Holy Spirit

As a child, I remember my pastor referring to the Holy Spirit as the Holy Ghost. I know I'm dating myself, but the cartoon series *Casper the Friendly Ghost*[2] came on every Saturday morning. I naturally thought the Holy Ghost must be very similar to Casper—just flying around out there. What a joy to discover he was so much more! John 14:16 tells us he's God himself, the Spirit of truth, and a Counselor to be with us forever. Jesus explained to the disciples that they knew the Holy Spirit because he lived with them. Even though Christ planned to leave the earth to return to his Father in heaven, he would return to them in the form of the Holy Spirit. From that time onward, he would be *in* them. And, wonder of wonders, he's within believers today. Imagine!

I was a senior at the University of Texas before I grasped that simple but basic truth. When I did, my walk with Christ changed dramatically. Realizing that the Holy Spirit was not floating around like Casper but residing inside me as a believer in Christ made a huge difference in my life. When I accepted by faith that Christ sent the Holy Spirit as my source of power to do and be all that he asked of me, I experienced such a wonderful freedom. In addition, my frustrated and fragmented walk with Christ slowly demonstrated more consistency. As a child, I asked Christ to forgive my sins and live within me. As a young adult, I asked the Holy Spirit who lived within me to cleanse, fill, and empower me as a follower of Christ. I think I can honestly say the joy I felt at that moment of yielding as a young adult was as significant as the joy and peace I experienced as a child when I first sought Christ's forgiveness.

Living an Obedient and Cleansed Life

I can remember my precious little granny explaining how she handled unkind thoughts about one of her friends. She said she just asked God to forgive her. If she didn't, she knew that with time she'd just end up being "a blowed-up-sucker." I can still remember my shock at discovering my Granny even had unkind thoughts! I assumed by the time you got that old, you were beyond such things. I've since learned we never truly reach a place in our spiritual journey when the Holy Spirit stops convicting us of areas not yet under the lordship of Christ. One of the most intimidating prayers I pray is, "Lord, is there something in my life you want me to see and deal with?" God always seems to answer this prayer. That's because he's in the lifelong process of making us "conformed to the likeness of his Son" (Rom. 8:29).

Secret sins, like resentment or unforgiveness, come from our sinful nature, and we can only deal with them success-fully by the power of the Holy Spirit. I was able to pray those prayers of "show me" only after I realized my own power-lessness to deal with heart sins. When I tried on my own to make the correction in behavior or attitude, I consistently failed. I could move beyond my negative attitudes and find release once I learned the Holy Spirit within me could re-place my resentment with his love. That freedom in Christ I'd sung about for years actually started becoming a reality. In addition, learning how to deal with disobedience and a rebellious heart freed me to begin hearing God's voice.

Hearing God's Word

The Holy Spirit not only convicts of sin but also reveals truth. Jesus told his disciples during that same discourse following the Passover meal that the Holy Spirit would "bring glory to me by taking from what is mine and making it known to you" (John 16:14). With time, the Holy Spirit revealed to the apostles the meaning of his death and resurrection. It's the Holy Spirit today who helps us understand these same truths recorded in God's Word. Have you discovered the power of God's Word in your life? In Hebrews 4:12, the writer describes God's Word as alive, active, penetrating, and sharp. Even the innermost parts of our personality and our thoughts cannot hide from it.

Bible study serves as a foundational area of women's ministry. We will explore ways to implement that later, but it's important on a personal level that we're each growing in our ability to hear God speak to us through his Word. It's the number one way he speaks to men and women today. His truths never change. His promises never change. His character never changes. The spiritual truths at the writing of each New Testament book remain true today. We can rely on his Word, trust it, and stand confidently on its power to transform our lives and the lives of women we serve. Learn to go there to hear God. His Word has the power to direct your steps, make or confirm a decision, reveal truth in a confusing world, set boundaries, accomplish the work of forgiveness, and even negotiate conflict. To be the driving force in women's ministry, his Word must first be the driving force in your own life.

Listening for God's Voice

I've heard many sermons on the still small voice or "gentle whisper" of God's voice when he spoke to the prophet Elijah in 1 Kings 19:9–13. God wasn't in the wind that passed by. He wasn't in the earthquake or the fire that followed. He was the "gentle whisper" that followed the fire. We're admonished to be still and listen to the gentle whisper of God's voice. We learn great truths in that biblical example, but it's also a pretty dramatic example of God communicating to one of his Old Testament prophets.

I don't know about you, but most of the time, I have found that hearing God turns out to be much less dramatic. When I hear God speak, it's usually through a gentle understanding, a thought, a truth of Scripture that grabs my attention, or a friend's encouraging word through an email, card, or phone call. Years ago, I came across a word picture in a song composed for pilgrims traveling up to Jerusalem. I've returned to that word picture again and again as I turn to God during a time of need.

> I lift up my eyes to you,
>   to you whose throne is in heaven.
> As the eyes of slaves look to the hand of their
>   master,
>   as the eyes of a maid look to the hand of her
>   mistress,
> so our eyes look to the LORD our God,
>   till he shows us his mercy.
>
> Psalm 123:1–2

This prayer acknowledges God as a God of provision for all needs. It also directs us to look to God for mercy. Many times I've found a quiet spot, sat down, looked upward, and waited. Most times I don't hear a thing from God in my spirit while I'm sitting there, but the experience stills my soul and communicates a heart attitude of listening. I always leave knowing God *will* communicate what I need to know in his perfect timing. He always has, and he will for you too.

Just as I discerned God's call on my life, I'm confident you too will hear God's voice through those you love, through God's Word, and through his Holy Spirit. The call and job description might vary from season to season or year to year. The position may be part-time, full-time, volunteer, or paid. You might work from your kitchen table at home or on the church campus. You might pioneer or follow behind someone else in leadership. Perhaps you'll head up the ministry, play a supportive role, or provide leadership for a specific ministry area. No matter what God calls you to do, you can feel confident you'll be able to discern God's will. The truth

Isaiah spoke to the children of Israel years ago remains true for believers in the twenty-first century: "Whether you turn to the right or to the left, your ears will hear a voice behind you, saying, 'This is the way; walk in it'" (Isa. 30:21).

For Reflection

1. When was the last time you paused to reflect on your spiritual walk? What did you discover?

2. After Christ left the earth, he promised to return in the form of the Holy Spirit and to indwell believers. How has understanding this indwelling personally empowered your walk with Christ?

3. In what areas of your life are you resisting God's authority? How will these unyielded areas affect your ability to lead women?

4. God most often speaks to me through a truth in Scripture, a thought, or a friend's encouraging word. How does God communicate to you?

3

Making the Choice

My righteous one will live by faith.

Hebrews 10:38

Mo noticed the desire for small group Bible studies among the women of her church and actively looked for ways to organize them. She also wanted to see the women involved in some special community outreaches. She and her husband had provided active leadership for many years in children's and youth ministries. Now Mo sensed God wanted her to focus on encouraging the women to grow further in their spiritual walk. She began visiting with women in leadership in other churches and seeking out equipping opportunities. Even though she juggled the activities of three teenagers, kept her eclectic antiques business afloat, and supported the demands of her husband's law practice, she still managed to find time to offer leadership to the women.

Look around in almost any church and you'll see those recently widowed or recently divorced, or those swamped with caring for elderly parents. You'll see bewildered new believers with spiritual questions and single moms praying their dollars will stretch to the end of the month. The resources to meet the needs of these women lie within each congregation, and God calls you to help him facilitate this very thing. Why do I know that? I believe God must have opened your eyes to see, your ears to hear, and your heart to feel women's needs or you wouldn't be taking time to read this book.

In the whirl of your own life, you've noticed women with hurts and women who need discipling. Priscilla, in the book of Acts, responded to needs in the early church by opening her home. She created an environment for other believers to grow. Dorcas ministered to widows by providing clothes for them. I'm confident she also offered friendship and emotional support. Their relationship with her was about much more than just clothing. God continues to multiply this same pattern of leadership among women in today's local church. In bodies of believers throughout your own city, women like Priscilla, Dorcas, and Mo are leading out to meet needs, to challenge, and to equip women. These women juggle all the demands of their personal world yet find time to respond to God's call on their life. God has guided each of their steps as they model a devoted lifestyle and challenge women to join them in reaching out to the women around them.

Mo expresses the thoughts of many other women like her: "I felt a longing to see God stir the hearts of the women in my church, so I began to pray God would lead me to those who had the same desire. I began to pray for God's leadership and to delve into God's Word. I talked with the church leadership and looked for ways to invite women to join me. Every step of the way I've felt anything but competent. I often wondered if God had made a mistake in calling me. Yet he's always been faithful in seeing me through my fears and insecurities and equipping me to face the challenges of leadership."

Finding Courage

Bruce Wilkinson says in *The Dream Giver* that many Christians misunderstand the emotion of fear. They believe if they were supposed to do this Big Dream, they wouldn't feel so afraid! They plan to wait until fear is gone before they take action. He says, "In my experience, God rarely makes our fear disappear. Instead, He asks us to be strong and take courage."[1] In reality, fear is simply an emotion that says, "Pay attention! You're about to do something you've never done before!" Fear doesn't disappear until we actually step out by faith, trusting in Christ's courage within us and beginning to feel comfortable with the new activities. Don't wait for the fear to go away. If God has nudged your heart, seek his guidance, then walk through any doors God opens for you. Admit that you feel faint of heart but you're trusting Christ to be courageous within you.

One morning I heard a teacher on a local Christian radio station describe courage.[2] He challenged the listeners to think of fear like those gates at the entrances of gated communities. The gate might look like a formidable barrier, but if you drive right up to it and wait, it opens automatically. He said to face fear the same way. Walk right up to it by faith and wait for God to make a way through. When you apply faith, God provides the courage and the way past the fear.

Taking Initiative

Building a ministry to women often begins with a journey of one. Over and over, I've heard women say they stepped out in faith when they felt they were the only ones seeing the need and hearing God's voice. They eventually discovered other women with similar desires to see God work, but not until they had begun their own journey. They initiated conversations with other women, times of prayer, meetings with church leadership, consultations with other women in church leadership, and training opportunities. They located financial resources for the training and invited other women to attend with them.

Before you start thinking I'm describing a machete-swinging, trailblazing woman, reconsider. She's much more like the biblical description of those disciples Jesus sent out, "shrewd as snakes and as innocent as doves" (Matt. 10:16). Demonstrating initiative means doing what needs to be done rather than waiting on someone else to do it. Here's an over-simplified example. When I'm in the neighborhood walking for exercise or even walking to my car in the church parking lot, I pick up any trash I pass. Occasionally someone asks why I bother. I simply respond, "Someone needs to, and it might as well be me!" I'm taking the initiative.

Once you begin a forward motion, Dr. Wilkinson also warns of naysayers. He describes what happens when you have an idea or dream and begin to take steps to make that dream a reality. Immediately, a variety of people offer opinions why you should not do this. He calls them "Border Bullies,"[3] people in our lives who say, "Turn back now!" We've all known them. I surely have. Dr. Wilkerson advises us to resist their negative messages and to persevere.

Seeking Discernment

Taking initiative requires prayerful discernment. Taking initiative at the wrong time or in the wrong way can be more detrimental than beneficial. Discernment and wisdom are both gifts from God. The Psalms and Proverbs offer examples of King David and King Solomon crying out to God for discernment and wisdom.

> "I, wisdom, dwell together with prudence; I possess knowledge and discretion" (Prov. 8:12).
> "The wisdom of the prudent is to give thought to their ways" (Prov. 14:8).
> "Wisdom reposes in the heart of the discerning" (Prov. 14:33).

"The discerning heart seeks knowledge" (Prov. 15:14).

Turn these truths into everyday prayers! Many times as a leader you'll feel clueless about the decisions you'll face. Call out to God for discernment. Let his Spirit nudge you in the right direction. Then, when the deadline arrives for the decision, you'll be at peace and ready to stand still or move forward, turn right or turn left. God will faithfully respond when you call out to him.

Developing Negotiation Skills

Sometimes making the choice to move forward in response to God's prompting requires negotiation skills. The Old Testament story of Abigail demonstrates brave and savvy negotiations with an angry King David. Abigail's drunken husband had "hurled insults" at David's men when they requested food. Abigail learned of David's plans of revenge and quickly devised a wise strategy to prevent bloodshed. Notice her negotiation skills. We read in 1 Samuel 25 that Abigail showed respect by falling at King David's feet when she intercepted him on a narrow mountain path. She asked permission to speak, saying, "I did not see the men my master sent" and "Please forgive your servant's offense" (vv. 25, 28). She provided the food King David initially requested from Nabal, then said in verse 28, "The LORD will certainly make a lasting dynasty for my master, because he fights the LORD's battles." Because of Abigail's skillful negotiations, King David recanted and no lives were lost. This particular story has an unusual twist at the end. Nabal died from an apparent stroke when Abigail told him how King David almost attacked—and King David took Abigail for his wife.

I remember the first negotiation of our fledgling women's ministry. Several young women in Bible study asked permission to add their children to the current Tuesday morning nursery. Our music ministry was already providing childcare for ensemble rehearsals that morning, but adding additional children required several meetings with the nursery coordinator and the educational minister to discuss funding and scheduling. An eventual "yes" rewarded patience and persistence.

I also like to read another Old Testament example of negotiation. Abraham actually negotiated with the Lord who arrived with two strangers. Abraham hoped to prevent the destruction of the cities Sodom and Gomorrah. I love that he wasn't afraid to ask for what he wanted. Too many times I falter and fail to make requests for specific needs in women's ministry. The early years of hearing "no" lulled me into a passive "why bother" attitude. During an annual review, my supervisor observed that I tended to assume former limitations were still in place when they actually were not. I didn't understand what he meant until I remembered an experiment from a psychology class at the University of Texas.

Fish swam in one half of a tank divided by a glass pane. The experimenters sprinkled fish food into the side opposite the fish and watched. They wanted to know how many bumps on the nose it took for the fish to give up attempting to reach the food. After the fish stopped trying, they removed the pane. The fish now had access to the food but no longer swam toward it. I realized I'd been behaving like the fish! Even though many of the constraints I'd worked under no longer existed, I still assumed they did. I wince at this additional thought: what if women throughout the body of Christ are holding back simply because they expect a "no" based on previous nos? If that's true, we've crippled the body of Christ just by our passivity.

If you've requested a beginning budget for women's ministry and been turned down, don't just give up. Ask, "What is the best time of the year to discuss budgets? May I reschedule a time to visit then?" Perhaps you're seeking assistance with childcare needs and don't feel as if you've made any progress. State, "We've noticed that a significant

41

number of women are unable to attend Bible study because of childcare needs. Can we discuss potential options for setting up childcare during Bible study?" During the negotiations, be ready to ask questions and offer suggestions: "If the women volunteered on a rotating basis to assist a paid worker, would that bring the nursery expense in line with budget limitations?" Or, "Is there a minimum fee we could charge the moms to be able to offer childcare?"

Women in leadership engage in simple negotiations day after day. It's part of the process of leadership. Learn to pay close attention to negotiation conversations and pick up pointers. Check with others for suggestions and creative alternatives to bring to your discussions. Contact other women in leadership for examples of how they handled a particular challenge. You'll typically discover just the bit of information you'll need to approach negotiations confidently. Remember, even though you might initially feel insecure, your skills will continue to increase and to improve with practice.

Resisting Discouragement

Discouragement doesn't mean you're on the wrong track or moving in the wrong direction. Discouragement might just mean you're tired or that you need to discover a fresh source of encouragement. Do you have a certain person who cheers you onward? If not, ask God to provide one.

What is your strategy for dealing with discouragement? My grandmother lost her husband in the early years of their marriage and raised eight children when her youngest, my father, was only two years old. She sold the farm in central Texas and built a boardinghouse with the proceeds. She had chickens and a garden in the backyard. She cooked meals for her college boarders on a wood-burning stove. I remember stories of how she coped with discouragement by pulling weeds in her garden. I don't know if pulling weeds is genetic or not, but I find myself outside pulling weeds in my flower beds when I feel discouraged. It just feels good to me. I get a sense of immediate reward and satisfaction. I also feel powerful and in control. Maybe it's the outside air and sunshine. Maybe it's just because I've laid my discouragements down for a time and refocused my energies. Develop your own strategy for coping. It will serve you well as you navigate the highs and lows of leadership.

Maintaining a healthy personal life to serve God will lengthen your leadership tenure and strengthen the effectiveness of your message to women. All of the responsibilities God places in your life, like marriage, motherhood, or caring for an aging parent, exist as multiple components of God's call on your life. Discovering how to integrate these demands with your limited time and energy provides healthy role modeling to others. It also sensitizes you to the challenges other women face.

Reflect upon what brings you pleasure. Mo McSwane collects all sorts of things and enjoys sharing her collections with friends. Her eyes twinkle as she points out favorites in her miniature dollhouse collection or explains why she still has her childhood toys on display. Maintaining hobbies and other outside interests energizes your days. Make time for them along with personal exercise and healthy eating. My husband purchased a bicycle for me four years ago. I ride around my neighborhood most mornings for exercise. The oxygen wakes me up and clears my head. I have no doubt that the days I ride are more productive than the days I don't ride. I truly have more energy. I'm often tempted to skip riding, but I realize that maintaining a healthy lifestyle provides the energy to respond to the other demands in my life.

Persevering

Women often ache within as they read about Hannah's barrenness and her prayer in the house of the Lord. Hannah, the mother of Samuel, knew how to persevere as she cried out to God for a son.

> In bitterness of soul Hannah wept much and prayed to the LORD. And she made a vow, saying, "O LORD Almighty, if you will only look upon your servant's misery and remember me, and not forget your servant but give her a son, then I will give him to the LORD for all the days of his life."
>
> 1 Samuel 1:10–11

Eli the priest saw Hannah's lips moving but didn't hear any words and presumed she'd had too much wine. Hannah replied, "I was pouring out my soul to the LORD. . . . I have been praying here out of my great anguish and grief" (vv. 15–16). Persist in prayer as you persevere in leadership. Trust God's timing for the working of his Spirit in the lives of the women in your church. Also trust God's timing in opening doors and making a way for the next stage of growth in women's ministry. Be encouraged by Hannah's own persistence. God honored hers and will honor yours.

For Reflection

1. The resources to meet the needs of women lie within each congregation. How is God calling you to help him facilitate this?

2. Prayer is one way to seek clarification of God's personal calling. What prayer has God laid on your heart?

3. Building a ministry to women often begins with one woman. What area of leadership do you feel God nudging you to investigate?

4. Discernment and wisdom are both gifts from God. In what specific areas do you sense a need for both?

4

ME, A LEADER?

Set an example for the believers in speech,
in life, in love, in faith and in purity.

1 Timothy 4:12

JOSETTE McCRARY
AND LOUISE POLLARD

Josette never planned on widowhood at the age of sixty-two, or at any age, actually. She faced the emotional losses of unfulfilled dreams and the daily emptiness at the kitchen table. The idea of a ministry to widows challenged her with a simple concept—monthly gatherings of widows for support and friendship. Josette hesitated until Louise offered to partner with her in leadership. Louise had felt called to minister to widows and eagerly offered her support. By fall, they launched a ministry offering encouragement and friendship to widows in their church and their community.

Josette's journey into leadership reflects a similar pattern in the lives of women God calls into leadership. In fact, it also parallels what we see in Scripture. In Genesis 18, we see Sarah eavesdropping on a conversation between her husband, Abraham, and three strangers. One of the guests, identified in Scripture as the pre-incarnate Christ, said, "I will surely return to you about this time next year, and Sarah your wife will have a son" (v. 10). Sarah doubted, saying to herself, "Will I really have a child, now that I am old?" (v. 13). I love the Lord's response in verse 14: "Is anything too hard for the LORD?" The same life-transforming change God produced in Sarah's life happens in the body of Christ every day. I'm not referring to conceiving past childbearing years but to something far more miraculous—moving from the anonymity of the crowd into leadership among women.

Three of the Gospels mention the women at the crucifixion scene watching and standing in the distance. In contrast, John mentions in chapter 19, "Near the cross of Jesus stood his mother, his mother's sister, Mary the wife of Clopas, and Mary Magdalene" (v. 25). These women had moved from the distant group closer to the cross. Roman soldiers typically allowed those in special relationship with the crucified to come close enough to hear their last dying words—equivalent to their last will and testament. These women found the courage to move out of the security of the crowd into the Roman spotlight. How I admire their vulnerability. How I admire the influence their presence has had on women through the past two thousand years.[1] That stepping forward is what you're doing in your journey of leadership. It's exactly what you'll be challenging other women to do when you invite them to join you in moving out of the obscurity of the crowd. It's often a frightening experience, though, and may require you to fearlessly confront what holds you back.

Things That Hold You Back

Maybe you dread the thought of speaking to a group of women. We're told speaking in front of crowds ranks right at the top of common sources of anxiety. Most of us automatically associate public speaking with leadership. We think of CEOs and politicians. We visualize someone standing in front of a lectern with a laser beam pointing to charts and graphs projecting budgets and future growth. Some women do thrive in that atmosphere, but many of the women God

47

calls into leadership find public speaking unfamiliar and frightening. Learn to befriend your feelings. Anxiety can become a companion that accompanies you rather than an adversary that attacks you. I know I have learned this. Eventually that uncomfortable feeling of doing something for the first time becomes so familiar it's no longer distracting.

Only the rarest of women travels through life unencumbered by the fear of failure. For the rest of us, it's a constant companion. We struggle with separating our actions from our selves. We believe that if what we do succeeds, then we're a successful person; if what we do fails, then we're a failure as a person. Neither premise is true. They're simply distortions of truth. Replace these thoughts with biblical realities: "If what I do succeeds, God accomplished it through me and I'll give him the praise and glory. If what I do fails, then I'll evaluate the experience, learn from it, and seek God's guidance for the next step." Even though you're familiar with making personal decisions about parenting, budgeting, and relationships, insecurities in decision making in women's leadership evoke fears of the public spotlight. Leadership decisions do become public decisions, but you can trust God's guidance in this new arena just like you trust him in the privacy of your home. God will be faithful to what he is calling you to do.

Do your reservations come from a poor self-image? How we see ourselves develops from our parents' earliest reflections to us. Their words became our personal mirror. Words like "You're such a good helper," "I love being with you," "I'm so glad you're my little girl" combine through the formative years to build a positive self-image. Women will often struggle with a negative self-image if they received mostly negative feedback like "Go away" or "Why can't you do anything right?" Asking God to begin the process of replacing these negative messages with his truth about you sets your feet on a healing journey. God's truths, like "You're my precious daughter whom I deeply love," will begin to permeate your heart. It will also begin to correct the poor self-image that holds you back from leadership.

Redefining Leadership

Gene Wilkes authored a Bible study entitled *Jesus on Leadership*.[2] It's helped many women inch out of the crowds because it redefines their concept of Christian leadership. Jesus didn't fit any of the profiles of CEO or politician. He did speak to crowds but usually in story format. He lived his life openly among them. He answered their questions. He addressed their fears and hurts. Christ lived his life as a servant. In fact, the term *servant-leadership* is now a part of many Christians' vocabulary. Christ led by being a servant. Remember the washing of the disciples' feet at the last Passover meal? Allow that to be your image of the leader God is calling you to be. It's an image to which most women can relate. We spend many of our waking and often-interrupted sleeping hours caring for and serving others. The difference in ministry to women is that you're inviting and equipping other women to do the same thing in a public way. When you ask, "Why would God ask *me* to do this?" answer your own question with "Why would he *not* ask me?" Is there a reason you're disqualified? God seeks out women with three basic qualifications: a faithful, believing walk; sensitivity to his Spirit; and availability to God. If you meet those criteria, you're qualified, and you can use those same criteria to invite other women to join you.

Understanding Leadership Basics

Women in the marketplace typically receive ongoing equipping in areas related to their responsibilities. They attend workshops to update their skills, including the lat-

49

est computer technology. Women who have not received this type of training and exposure often feel overwhelmed with the thought of assuming leadership responsibilities. Dr. Thomas McGaffey distills the complexity of leadership to the basics of leading through the conversations we have with others.[3] Rather than thinking of leading through formal meetings with agendas, we simplify our concept of leading to focused conversations we have in the hallways, over the phone, or even through emails or text messages. It's a great strategy for women in leadership, because women and conversations are an unbeatable combination!

As a woman leading other women, you'll engage in discussions that move someone to action ("I'd love to see you do this"), foster trust ("I have confidence you can do this"), and inspire personal growth ("Would you share what you've learned with Erin over coffee?"). Other conversations will solve problems ("Let's figure out what went wrong") and establish goals ("What do you think we should set as attendance goals?"). Leaders learn to separate casual conversations from those that have a specific and purposeful objective. Relax! As a woman, you're already adept at connecting with other women through conversations. As a leader, you just decide on the objective you want to accomplish through that conversation.

Discovering Your Leadership Style

Reflect on the people around you, and you'll probably discover that those people bring distinctively different approaches to leadership. Gregarious or outgoing women typically lead through a cheerleading, you-can-do-it style. Strong-willed women bring a direct and opinionated get-the-job-done style of leadership to their responsibilities. Easygoing personalities offer a steadiness and a calming approach to their ministry areas. Reflective personalities offer good, solid information for those they lead. The whole point of these leadership styles is that you can do it *your way*! There's not just one way to lead. Don't try to duplicate someone else's personality. Be yourself. Lead the way God created you to lead.

Two additional leadership styles oppose one another. One breeds resentment. The other builds enthusiasm and ownership. I refer to them as *top-down* and *bottom-up leadership*. Top-down leaders tell others what to do and how to do it. They want accountability and control. They micromanage. The results look great for a while, but there's little ownership and a high level of turnover in volunteers under this type of leadership. These volunteers feel they're there just "to get the job done." Often the leader gets the credit for all their hard work. In bottom-up leadership, you'll see a lot of independent decision making and input from the volunteer base. They take ownership because they have ownership and they're quick to assume more responsibilities. It's an environment that produces strong leaders and strong ministries.

Understanding Those You Lead

Women bring certain strengths to their leadership. Intuition and empathy head the list. *Intuition* expresses itself as a form of instinctive knowing without the use of the conscious reasoning process. It's information that comes from observations that you're not aware of taking in. Many of the personality indicators actually use "intuition" as one of their diagnostic tools for temperament. Even though some people have higher levels of intuitive ability, all individuals can learn to trust their intuition and continue to develop their intuitive skills.

Empathy, on the other hand, involves more of a choice. You choose to place yourself in the other woman's shoes and think about her feelings or her perspective. An empathetic response to the challenges and frustrations of those you lead helps to communicate you care. Even if you haven't walked in their shoes, you can mentally place yourself in their situation and think about how you'd respond. Viewing life from their perspective is a good place to be when God prompts you to offer grace, forgiveness, or correction.

Just like intuition, you can grow in empathetic abilities. Reading, listening, and firsthand experiences broaden your understanding of another's reality. Several years ago I had the privilege of attending a workshop entitled "Understanding Poverty Thinking."[4] I learned how people in each economic level possess identifiable belief systems. I've been surprised since the training at how clearly I can now see those beliefs in action. The same principles also apply to leading others. Listening and understanding the whys behind their decisions helps me feel less judgmental even when I disagree with choices they make. God's begun the work in my heart of learning how to extend acceptance of those I'm leading.

No other individual ministry in the local church spans as many seasons of life and lifestyle choices as women's ministry. I interact almost daily with very diverse women. Stay-at-home moms, homeschooling moms, private- and public-schooling moms, single moms, divorced women, marketplace women, empty nesters, grandmothers, retirees, and widows. Wow! Isn't that an amazing assortment? We'll discuss the challenges of addressing the needs of each group at a later point. For now, let's think about how you can understand those you lead. Actually, apart from the Holy Spirit providing insight, you can't! But you can observe women in each season and style of life. You can listen to their personal challenges, and you can ask questions when you need clarification. I remember the most amazing question that popped out of my mouth several summers ago.

Kitty, a homeschooling mother of five, arrived for a summer Bible study with a broad smile. She announced, "Finally, summer is here. It's my turn to study!" I noticed the exhaustion in her voice and on her face. That's when I asked that surprising question, "How can Women's Ministry support you in what you feel God has called you to do?" Kitty stood there wide-eyed and finally said, "I'll have to think about that"—and she did. That fall we set aside a room during our weekday morning Bible study for five homeschooling moms and their children. They brought their kids and provided joint activities while the women enjoyed fellowship and support with one another. I didn't have to be a homeschooling mom to see and respond to the needs of homeschooling moms. I only had to observe and respond. That's all you'll need to do too.

Assembling a Leadership Team

Your *leadership team* serves a dual purpose. They represent their peer group, but they also become your personal accountability group. These women will provide a sounding board whenever you drift off course. They'll offer their spiritual gifts and life experiences to influence decisions, directions, and anything they see that might concern them. Just last week I had a member of my leadership team share a concern. She felt the leadership team reflected mostly "mature" women—ranging from thirties to early sixties. She felt we needed a professional woman in her twenties on board, and she stated her reason—we needed to intentionally mentor the next generation who will bring their life skills and resources into church leadership. I immediately thought of all the difficulties of locating someone with that profile when God interrupted. Putting together a leadership team is God's responsibility, not mine. So I stopped my mental complaining, prayed, and asked him to guide us to that new team member. In this particular instance, the new team member actually contacted me, asking about opportunities to serve in the women's ministry. She had two small children and worked part-time in real estate out of her home. Meeting monthly and representing her peer group met our needs and her schedule perfectly.

Build in financial accountability by including a review of the current finances during your leadership meetings no matter how small the account. Encourage each member of the leadership team to ask about allocation of funds, purchases, etc. The church financial office provides additional accountability, but your leadership team influences the direction and priorities of the budget.

Your team also assists with setting purpose statements and plans for the future. That prevents you from using your position of leadership to accomplish personal agendas instead of agendas for the women of the church. They can also help evaluate ideas and opportunities to see if they align with the ministry's purpose. As time passes, you'll stand amazed at the diversity of what God is doing through the women of your church. Time with the leadership team allows you to summarize what's happened the previous month and what's on tap for the upcoming months. It will feel good to know that at least a few others besides yourself are informed about what's happening.

Developing Guidelines for Team Members

Your leadership style influences your expectations of your team. Some leaders prefer that their teams sign commitment agreements for a set length of time and then rotate off. Others ask their team members to be sensitive to the Holy Spirit and trust him to tell them when he has other responsibilities for them. Some leaders feel strongly about punctuality and consistent attendance. Others ask members to prioritize their schedules around their monthly meetings and make three-fourths of the yearly meetings. They also try to accommodate the external time demands their working women face. Some members have specific assigned responsibilities while others simply represent their peer group and participate in some area of work with women. We all wish for a manual with clear-cut guidelines for "how to organize and lead your leadership team." Women are far too diverse for a one-size-fits-all approach. Examine the team member guidelines in appendix 2 and use it as a springboard for designing your own. How you choose to organize and resource your team leaders will flow out of your own leadership needs. The shape and expectations of the team will grow and develop right along with you and the ministry.

Growing in Leadership Skills

My mother taught high school homemaking, raised four kids, and checked her much-loved Charolais cattle every morning and evening, yet she always had time to read any book we'd bring home from college. She enjoyed continuing to learn right along with us. Learning about leading is a never-ending journey filled with adventures and challenges. Ask other women in leadership about their favorite resources. I creased the binding on a ninety-day devotional book called *Women in Leadership.*[5] As I drew from other women's journeys, I felt encouraged, understood, and mentored—I knew I wasn't alone. My worn edition of Oswald Chambers's classic, *My Utmost for His Highest,*[6] keeps me reflecting on the innermost working of personal spiritual growth. I hope I never leave his book behind. Ask other women in leadership to recommend their favorite resource and begin building a personal library of dog-eared and highlighted "friends." One of my favorite authors quoted Steinbeck, describing one of his character's love for reading: "But Tom got into a book, crawled and groveled between the covers, tunneled like a mole among the thoughts, and came up with the book all over his face and hands."[7] That's how I've read some of my mentoring resources. Search until you find one that you enjoy as much as Tom did!

Look for training opportunities in addition to building your library. Professional seminars address things like conflict resolution, public speaking, office organization, and a wide variety of other topics. The cost is minimal compared to the information you'll receive and be able to apply in your new responsibilities. State-licensed professions require ongoing education. Ask those in the helping professions about workshops and seminars they plan on attending, and consider joining them. Websites of ministries like Kimberly Chastain's Coaching,[8] Christa.net,[9] and Leadership Network[10] offer online resources for leadership coaching. Simulcasts[11] available through your area churches can also provide excellent equipping seminars.

Several years ago women expressed the desire for women-friendly leadership training to Rhonda Kelly, the wife of the New Orleans Baptist Seminary president. She, in turn, mentioned it to her husband. He responded with,"Let's start a Women's Leadership Certificate program." The program now offers basic and advanced certificates. Other seminaries have begun to offer this option plus master's and doctoral degrees with an emphasis in women's sudies. These new and exciting opportunities for women did not even exist ten years ago.

Paul wanted the believers in Thessalonica to know what he prayed for them. Paul wrote in 2 Thessalonians 1:11–12, "We constantly pray for you, that our God may count you worthy of his calling, and that by his power he may fulfill every good purpose of yours and every act prompted by your faith. We pray this so that the name of our Lord Jesus may be glorified in you, and you in him, according to the grace of our God and the Lord Jesus Christ." I'm praying the same for you today. God is ready to provide whatever you need to serve him effectively—that he may be glorified.

Building a Support Team

For years I've sat in worship noticing the gray-haired ladies and picking the ones I want to look like when I reached their age. They're the ones who sing, laugh, and generally have eyes that twinkle. These precious ladies mentor me just by their presence. They've lived a life filled with both joys and hardships, and they've learned the grace of perseverance. Their firsthand experience can never be replaced by a book I might read. Ask God to direct you to a personal mentor, intercessor, and confidant. Take the initiative in creating a personal network for growing as a leader.

You can also find women mentors via the Internet for questions and encouragement. Jennifer Rothschild has developed a monthly email for women's ministry leadership filled with creative ideas and networking opportunities.[12] Visit church websites for contacts for women's ministry, then take the time to contact them by email or by phone with your questions. If they don't know the answer to your questions, they'll be able to put you in touch with someone who does.

Make the effort to discover women in leadership in area churches and begin to network. Get together regularly for "lunch and laughter." Just begin enjoying one another as friends. Eventually, you'll also begin sharing resources and training opportunities. You might even schedule a road trip to a training conference together and share expenses. It's a great learning and bonding experience. You'll be a source of encouragement for one another as well as a source of peer mentoring. You'll have an opportunity to talk about your concerns, frustrations, dreams, and challenges. The exchange of information will enhance your leadership skills by providing a support system to undergird and strengthen you as a leader.

⚭

As you move out of the crowd and begin your journey into leadership, deal proactively with those uncomfortable feelings of tackling new and unfamiliar responsibilities. As you move forward in faith, the Lord will provide equipping resources at just the right time and just as you need them. Developing a leadership team provides accountability for you as a leader and also creates an environment for passing on what you're learning. It's a great strategy for duplication! It's a shared journey with amazing surprises as more and more women join you in the process of growing as leaders.

One of the next opportunities you'll face will be developing partnering skills with other members of your church leadership team.

For Reflection

1. Only the rarest of women travel through life unencumbered by the fear of failure. For the rest of us, it's a constant companion. What is one of your greatest fears?

2. Christ lived his life among his followers as a servant. He led from a servant's heart. In what ways will this be difficult or come naturally for you?

3. Reflect on a variety of Christian women leaders and note their leadership styles. Whose style do you most closely identify with?

4. Women bring certain strengths to their leadership. Intuition and empathy are two strengths. What strengths do you feel you can bring to leadership?

PART II

HEADING FORWARD
IN FAITH

Leadership will challenge you to new levels of spiritual growth as you begin to learn and practice the relational skills of a leader. You'll discover a rich diversity of women already serving in the church as you begin to network these ministries with one another and with new church members. You'll also experience the joy of watching other women mature in leadership skills as they begin meeting needs of others.

5

LAUNCHING OR EXPANDING
A MINISTRY

His compassions never fail. They are new every morning;
great is your faithfulness.

Lamentations 3:22–23

LAURA JOHNSON

Laura moved a thousand miles to a state and town that felt to her like the frontier of civilization. She and her husband both longed for the friends and fellowship of their former church. Laura began to combat her loneliness by finding a church home and investigating opportunities for Bible study with the women. She eventually located ten interested women. Through the support of her former church's women's ministry, Laura was able to begin introducing women to the joys of studying God's Word together.

L aura left her previous church as a *participant* in women's ministry. In her new church, Laura took the initiative to organize women in Bible study. She moved into a *leadership* role. Leaders like Laura will begin to seek out other women to serve beside them. You'll consistently ask as a leader, "How can I connect with other women called to leadership? How do I identify those with the same heartbeat? I know they're out there; I just don't know how to find them." The answer is always the same—ask God. Ask him to lead you to women who have the same desire to see God begin working in the hearts of women.

Praying Together

As God clarifies your dream, begin to share it with other women—whether it's over tea, at a coffee shop, or via email. Ask them if they'll join you in regular prayer times asking for God's leadership. Jesus gave the disciples a pattern for prayer in response to their request, "Lord, teach us to pray, just as John taught his disciples" (Luke 11:1). He responded by speaking to God with the tenderness of a child, calling him "Father." He also modeled holy respect when he prayed, "Father, hallowed be your name" (v. 2). The prayer recorded in Matthew includes a request: "your will be done on earth as it is in heaven" (Matt. 6:10). Christ asks for God's will on earth now, just as it always exists in heaven. That's exactly what we as leaders want—God's will.

Jesus continues his teaching on prayer with a parable of knocking on a neighbor's door late at night. Today we'd probably call instead, but in simpler times a determined person would continue to knock until someone answered the door. I've had the privilege of sharing in a ministry that began fifteen years ago with three women who met regularly for prayer. They'd seen the diversity of needs among the women and longed to find a way to address them. They simply prayed that God would make a way—and they continued to pray for three years before a door finally opened. "Ask and it will be given to you; seek and you will find; knock and the door will be opened to you. For everyone who asks receives; he who seeks finds; and to him who knocks, the door will be opened" (Luke 11:9–10).

Consider this mental picture when you pray. See yourself seeking out God's house, knocking on his front door, and asking for the desires of your heart. Bruce Wilkinson says in *The Dream Giver*, "You have been handcrafted by God to accomplish a part of His Big Dream for the world. How? Your Big Dream is meant to fulfill a Big Need He cares deeply about. The reason you're here is to take a part of His Dream from Point A to Point B."[1] Begin a prayer list of desires, the topics you want to pray about, like leadership of the Holy Spirit, the staff's support, responses from other women, and open doors. Pray for mentors who can answer questions and offer guidance in your journey. Ask, seek, knock, and the door will open.

Meeting with the Pastor

After laying the foundation of prayer, you'll want to meet with the pastor for permission and guidance. You'll create a wonderful opportunity to gain his support and to receive valuable insight. We'll discuss working with church leadership in a future chapter, but for now, this initial contact communicates your willingness to work within the parameters of his pastoral guidance. Ask for a brief meeting to discuss options for ministering to the women of the church. What women typically take thirty to forty-five minutes to communicate, a man can accomplish in ten to fifteen—so prepare ahead of time. Bring a summary of what you want to say and leave a copy with him. In this initial meeting, you'll just want to address the vision of what women's ministry can bring to the body of Christ.[2] Be ready to share your thoughts on such things as financial or childcare needs as well as names of other women available to help. Even though you're thinking about what God can accomplish through the ministry, your pastor might also be ready to discuss such things as facilities usage, childcare costs, how this new ministry fits into the overall church goals, and which minister can take on an additional area of supervision.

Your pastors will also have questions about you as a leader. Don't let this intimidate you. It's logical to assume he'll want to know if you demonstrate consistency in your spiritual walk and can work well with church leadership. What seems so simple to you might not seem so simple to him. Beyond sharing your vision for women's ministry, you'll want to ask for permission to conduct a survey. Be sure to offer to share the results with him. Remember, this initial meeting is to lay the groundwork for the vision of women's ministry and to let the pastor know how God is working in your heart, not a time to present a brainstorming list of possible programs. Be sure to take a pen and paper and write down any question you can't answer and assure him you'll get back to him with the information.

Don't be surprised if you're in and out of the meeting in under fifteen minutes. Most pastors respond positively when they see how a ministry to women strengthens and expands the work of the church.[3] Trust God to make a way. God will guide your pastor—the very one God charged with shepherding you and the rest of the congregation. Whatever the response, God is in control and you can trust his timing.

Doing Your Homework

Asking for feedback from the women in your church allows you to design a ministry that meets the needs in your church. There's no such thing as a cookie-cutter ministry. Each ministry has a unique profile. That's because the needs of women vary from church to church. Some churches have a high percentage of working women. Others have a large population of retirees. Suburban churches often reflect young families living in the community. The structure of each ministry needs to reflect the unique needs of each of these groups.

You'll want to know three basics: (1) Do the women of the church want a women's ministry? (2) What are their felt needs? (3) Who has the desire to assist with leadership? Consider including additional questions about times they'd be available for Bible study. Will they need childcare? What length of study do they prefer—four weeks, eight weeks, or twelve weeks? Have they had experience in facilitating a study, and what are their particular topics of interest? Check appendix 4 for a sample survey you can reproduce, or consider designing your own so you can tailor it to meet your specific needs. You can also format a survey for specific situations. For instance, will you ask the questions orally and record the answers, or will you distribute them for women to write out their own answers? Do you want them to choose between options or to suggest their own ideas? Do you want names, addresses, cell phone numbers, and emails, or do you want the info to be anonymous?

Here's a surveying rule of thumb: the shorter the survey, the larger the response. So, select your questions carefully and then decide on when and where you'll distribute them. Some women have found that offering a Hershey's kiss along with a smile and a request for two minutes of their time on a Sunday morning at church gets good results. Others have found that compiling surveys online or using email provides a convenient way to access busy women. If your church has a website, you can even post a few questions there and ask for a response. Young moms might participate in a brief phone survey after the kids have gone to bed. A professional might be willing to meet you for lunch or give you feedback during a morning coffee break. Take into account the unique profile of your church's membership, and be creative. God will give you the information you'll need to provide for on-target planning.

Finding a Mentor

I love to experiment with a variety of plants in my flower beds. I investigate plants at the gardening center, and I ask friends for cuttings or seeds from their gardens. I read articles and consult with like-minded friends. I even subscribe to email gardening newsletters to learn from questions other gardeners ask. I've sought a variety of mentors to help me grow in my skills as a gardener. As a result, I've learned why the willow transplant from the mountains of northern New Mexico hasn't thrived in my East Texas flower bed. I've also discovered how to naturally decrease my population of snails and June bugs. Locating a mentor for leading a women's ministry will help your leadership and the ministry grow. Perhaps an older, wiser woman right in your church could provide wise counsel. Don't be discouraged if you need to look beyond your church or even to another city to find a mentor. Seek God's leading, and he'll direct you to her.

Trusting God's Timing

I'm sure you've heard the phrase, "God's timing is always perfect." It's true! Multiple reasons might influence the pastor to ask you to delay the "launch." Overextended budgets, a staff vacancy, a building campaign, or other reasons might affect the pastor's decision. Be patient. Continue to pray and ask to visit with him again in six months. I love the profile the writer of Hebrews paints concerning guidelines in these situations. "Obey your leaders and submit to their authority. They keep watch over you as men who must give an account. Obey them so their work will be a joy, not a burden, for that would be of no advantage to you" (Heb. 13:17).

I often write special verses in the back of my Bible along with a note or two concerning the occasion. In July 2001, I recorded Hebrews 13:17 and wrote "good directive for women in leadership." This verse provided just the admonition I needed to bring my attitude into God's design for the church. I needed to remember that leaders God places over us must give account to God. They have weighty responsibilities, and I can trust God's sovereignty in placing them there. I particularly appreciated the additional admonition—

making their responsibilities burdensome would not benefit me in any way! A women's ministry in the church should be a joy, not a burden! It doesn't get any clearer than that! Memorize Hebrews 13:17, then place it on your bathroom mirror as a constant reminder. Allow God to use it to bring you into his design for ministry.

As you discover ways to share your dream with other women and church leadership, you'll uncover a variety of stretching opportunities. Mentors, prayer, and faith in God's timing will put in place new leadership skills God can build upon in the adventurous months ahead.

For Reflection

1. As God clarifies your dream, share it with other women and invite them to join you in regular prayer times seeking God's leadership. Name two to three women you might invite to pray with you.

2. Asking for feedback from the women in your church allows you to design a ministry that meets their needs. What type of information would you like to know?

3. Trusting God's timing is an act of faith. In what areas do you need patience?

4. As a leader, you'll experience a variety of growth opportunities. In what areas do you feel God is stretching you?

6

SHARING THE VISION

I will do whatever you ask in my name,
so that the Son may bring glory to the Father.

John 14:13

CONNIE HUNSLEY

Connie enjoyed the playful early years of parenting her three girls. She later taught science to eighth graders to assist with the girls' college expenses. After the two oldest girls graduated, Connie decided to leave the classroom and investigate ministry opportunities in the community and in her local church. She attended a women's leadership conference and rejoiced to discover how ministry to women had expanded. As she reviewed possibilities for ministry in her church, her heart jumped at the idea of reaching out to single moms. As a young mother, she'd watched the devastation as a close friend coped with the unexpected crisis of divorce and single parenting. The experience had sensitized her to the hurts and challenges of single moms. She knew she wanted to reach out with support, guidance, and encouragement. After visiting with church leadership about the need, she launched the Single Mom Connection.

For many years I've sat where I can pray over Sunday morning worshipers and ask God to call out women to serve him. I like to observe women's interactions with their children or husbands. I notice their weariness, their elderly parents, or the loneliness of widowhood—the stages and phases of women's lives. It's become second nature to look for the faces of women in the crowded aisles or hallways. Eye contact and a smile communicates that you're approachable for conversation, for an encouraging word, or to answer a visitor's question—each an opportunity for connecting. My heart leaps when I imagine the untapped gifts and life experiences within each one. I marvel at what would happen in the kingdom of God if each woman responded to God's call on her life. I then consider how to personally be a part of that process.

Expanding the dream of women reaching out to women in the church and beyond requires talking and connecting with other women. Ask questions both informally and formally. I've discovered a comfortable format I've named "Tea & Talk." It began with my friend and cohort, Nancy Paul, a true-blue, tea-drinking Canadian. She not only enjoys her tea midmorning and midafternoon but also prefers cream, scones, and lemon curd with her tea. As we worked together on projects, Nancy always stopped for tea breaks and I'd join her. Soon, I offered women a cup of tea when they stopped by to visit, to plan, or just to touch base. I located a small round tea table at a flea market, and it didn't take long before teatime turned into "Tea & Talk." Soft drinks, coffee, or bottled water accomplish the same purpose of providing an opportunity to pursue dreams and clarify expectations. If women know they have your attention and feel accepted unconditionally, they'll freely share their struggles and their dreams. Within that context, you'll not only discover their heart but will also establish a heart connection.

Paying Attention

Besides becoming a tea drinker, I've also become an eavesdropper. Anytime women gather, I listen. I pay attention to their conversations and their laughter. I pay attention when someone is expressing passionate feelings or concerns—whether it's a church, a community, or a national concern. Are they discussing caregiving stressors, challenges with teenagers, or grief issues? Are they expressing unmet personal needs or noting needs around them? What's uppermost on their minds? What is the source of their passion? Sometimes I join the conversation. By observing and interacting, I feel more aware of what impassions a woman. A key element of building a ministry to women is doing just that—connecting with women where they live.

Getting in Touch

Occasionally women feel out of touch with their personal interests or passions. Perhaps they're simply numbed by the relentless demands of life. Maybe they're just too busy taking care of others. I'll never forget my husband asking what kind of cake I wanted for my fortieth birthday. I answered, "Well, Lisa likes Angel Food with whipped icing. Jonathan likes carrot cake, Nathan likes cinnamon streusel cake, and Lori likes chocolate cake." Gary interrupted me with "I asked what kind *you* liked." I discovered I didn't even know! When women repeatedly set aside their needs to respond to the needs of others, they can lose touch with who they are by God's design. Effective leaders will help them to rediscover their passions. In rediscovering their passions, women might also discover they're God's woman for addressing this need in someone else's life—just like God uses Connie Hunsley and her sister-in-law, Linda, in blessing single moms. Connie rediscovered the deep feelings she had from years past watching her friend struggle as a single mother. Now she actually had an opportunity to use that passion to make a difference in someone else's life.

Fortunately, we now have a variety of excellent resources for women to begin this process of self-discovery. Sometimes simply brainstorming with them provides significant clues. Watch their body language and their eyes. When you touch upon a topic they feel passionate about, they'll sit up straighter, perhaps lean forward, and begin monopolizing the conversation! Their eyes twinkle, and they'll hold your gaze. Use these clues to pursue this particular topic. I saw this recently in conversation with my friend Margie. As she and I visited, she became animated as she spoke about the need to encourage caregivers. She sat up straighter, talked faster, and began to use her hands as she spoke. This coming spring will mark the one-year anniversary of Margie meeting monthly with caregivers in the church for Bible study and prayer.

Asking Others

Learn how to ask for the information you need for leading women. Ask until you locate a church with an active women's ministry. Ask the leader about your questions or concerns. She'll provide a valuable source of encouragement when you feel disheartened and information when you feel clueless! Our own "founding women" located a church with a women's ministry within eighty miles. They made a day trip and established connections with women that later served to cheer and encourage when times got tough. It's just amazing how simple words like "We went through the same thing" or "Growing pains are normal" can renew your spirit and keep you moving forward. Even if you never meet your mentor face-to-face and have to depend on emails and phone calls, you'll be blessed by the valuable assistance as you move forward in faith.

Wherever you are in this journey, whether it's finding someone to pray with you or to tally the results of the surveys, you're right on schedule. God has a wonderful design he wants to implement within your particular body of believing women, and he'll guide you each step of this exciting journey.

For Reflection

1. Expanding the dream of women reaching out to women in the church and beyond requires connecting with other women. What are some opportunities at your church for asking for input from the women about their needs and interests?

2. Observing women provides a wealth of information helpful to you as a leader: note family members, stage of life, physical disabilities, interests, etc. What are some opportunities for you to observe women at your church?

3. Listen to women when they gather with one another. Pay attention to their conversations. What are some of the dominant concerns among the women of your church right now?

4. Learn how to ask for the information you need for leading women. Locate a church with an active women's ministry. Contact the leader about your questions or concerns. What is the number one question you'd like to ask someone right now?

7

TALKING SO MEN WILL UNDERSTAND

Love is patient, love is kind. It does not envy,
it does not boast, it is not proud. It is not rude,
it is not self-seeking, it is not easily angered.

1 Corinthians 13:4–5

Rachel Bitter

Rachel divides her internship between the singles' minister and the women's minister. She says, "Working for both a man and a woman has allowed me to become bilingual. As I navigate my daily responsibilities, I am constantly switching between the two different languages in order to communicate more effectively. When communicating to the singles' minister, I've learned to speak directly and in a respectful manner. I bring him just the information he needs to know. He never asks for extra details. In working with the women's minister, I get to share background information, any interesting details, and even how I feel."

Most women have read several books on understanding the male mind and have picked up some helpful insights. I remember my surprise when I learned I needed extra study to communicate in the work environment. Reading books on marriage communication didn't necessarily translate to the workplace! Working relationships have different goals and parameters. Through experience, books, trial and error, and my husband's wise counsel, I've learned many valuable lessons that help me communicate with men on the church leadership team.

Women generally use more words than men and speak on a feeling level. Men typically use fewer words and speak on a factual level. Of course these are only generalities, but knowing common principles can improve effective communication, especially with the church staff member who supervises you. One effective resource I've found is *Mars and Venus in the Workplace*[1] by John Gray. He does a super job of describing some common sources of miscommunication among men and women in the workplace. One helpful insight I immediately put into practice with my supervisor dealt with asking up front to "talk through my thoughts." That helps him understand how I communicate. If I take longer than usual, I've also learned to express appreciation for his time and to acknowledge that his listening offered constructive assistance. He, in turn, has a sense that his time was used wisely and not wasted. This small bit of office etiquette creates a win-win situation.

Thinking out loud is different from circular talking. Circular talkers include background information in story form before they "circle around" to their point. They believe adding all the details engages the listener. This might hold true for their women friends, but not for the average male. Even circular talkers can learn to state their request or make their point first. They can save the details of the story or the steps leading to their conclusion for another time. It requires personal discipline, but the rewards are worth it. Men will feel you value their time and will offer it more freely.

Identifying Our Preconceptions

I've learned that we bring our personal preconceptions about men into our work relationships. My father had an explosive temper, and I always felt vulnerable and powerless around him. I quickly realized that to be an effective communicator, I needed to put aside my little-girl fears and remain mentally engaged in the presence of men who might occasionally talk loudly or even express anger. I've learned to move past those vulnerable feelings and look for the appropriate time to communicate with calm confidence. Along with occasional loud voices, men tend to "shoot straight" and "move on" while women tend to "speak indirectly" and "hold grudges." I'm learning to speak directly and not hold grudges when I don't get the response I'm seeking. You can too.

Women often tend to interpret a man's "grumbling" as whining. As a mom, I know whining when I hear it. While recently visiting on the phone with my daughter Lisa, I could hear my two-year-old granddaughter making a strange noise in the background. When I asked about it, Lisa explained, "It's nothing. Isabella is just moaning. No, she's not sick or in pain, she's just moaning." A short time later, it hit me. Isabella was whining, not moaning. I called my daughter back within the hour. This first-time mother needed to quickly implement the rule I grew up with—no whining allowed!

Imagine my surprise when I learned that men's grumbling is not an adult form of whining. Grumbling means something entirely different in male-speak. It means, "I'm going to do what you ask, but this is an inconvenience, and I want you to appreciate my effort." Wow. I no longer shy away from the grumblers when I need something, and I make sure to express my appreciation for their effort.

Getting the Job Done

My husband's pet peeve is how women perceive him at work. His female co-workers sometimes interpret his focus on "getting the job done" as being too job focused and not enough people focused. He also experiences frustration with women who respond with compassionate actions but lack discernment in the best way to respond. He believes that taking time to get all the facts might lead them to a different response. I fit his female co-workers' profile! I felt like he was describing my actions and thoughts toward some of my own male co-workers, especially those who oversee benevolence needs. I'm learning to gather as many facts of the situation as possible and to clarify the specific need before I submit it. I've also learned that men's probing questions don't indicate insensitivity but thoughtful stewardship of God's resources.

Recently a distraught woman came by the women's office asking for bus fare to New Orleans and money to cover three nights' lodging. The city officials had notified her that they had uncovered her daughter's body from the debris of Hurricane Katrina. They needed her to return and provide DNA identification. Her wailing and mourning deeply moved many of the women arriving for Bible study. The local newspaper article she clutched confirmed she had cared for her five-year-old grandson during the past year while waiting to hear of her daughter's fate. It was 8:30 a.m. and that day's bus left at 10:00 a.m. There was no time to run this need through normal benevolence channels. The women graciously met her financial needs. When I shared the story with the minister in charge of benevolence, I was mentally prepared to receive his objective guidance for responding wisely to emotional emergencies. He counseled, "You might have asked her to come by your office after she returned from New Orleans and to turn in receipts for her expenses. That would have allowed you to be part of the emotional follow-up as well as providing a moderate form of accountability." That was wise counsel! I've learned that objective male thought and emotional female responses can combine to enhance the church's response to needs around us.

Lysa TerKeurst of Focus on the Family Ministries reminds women working alongside men that "it's to your advantage to remain feminine"[2] and to draw upon your strong relational skills. When things go awry, she suggests you ask yourself these questions: Have I been prepared for meetings? Have I been overly emotional with the church leadership so they have to walk on eggshells when they talk to me? Do I take criticism personally, or do I use it to build a better program? Every day offers a new learning opportunity in working with the opposite gender, so continue to grow as you equip yourself with effective communication strategies.

For Reflection

1. In working with men in church leadership, you'll face the challenge of gender-specific styles of communication. What is one gender communication issue you've already encountered?

2. We bring our preconceptions about men into our work relationships. What are some preconceptions you have about communicating with men?

3. Many times, women view a man's focus of "getting the job done" as lacking sensitivity to others. How does "getting the job done" actually serve people?

4. Lysa TerKeurst of Focus on the Family Ministries reminds women working alongside men to remain feminine and to draw upon their relational skills. In what ways do you see your relational skills benefiting your leadership? Review Lysa's questions in the last paragraph. What personal blind spot did you discover?

8

PARTNERING WITH CHURCH LEADERSHIP

But the fruit of the Spirit is love, joy, peace, patience, kindness, goodness, faithfulness, gentleness and self-control. Against such things there is no law.

Galatians 5:22–23

When Lesa began serving as the women's ministry director, she felt cautious about her new responsibilities. She asked specifically about anything that related to women's ministry. She watched and learned and eventually became an interactive team member. She reflects on those awkward first weeks as she learned how the team worked together. She appreciates and enjoys the camaraderie that eventually developed between her and the staff. She's so glad she persevered through the challenging early days.

Joining the church staff as a volunteer, part-time worker, or full-time worker launches a wonderful new season of personal growth. Weekly meetings or informal conversations will all bring new adventures as you learn personalities and policies. You'll discover both written and unwritten guidelines. Expect to learn most of the unwritten ones by asking or by trial and error. Consider the insecure feeling of "I don't know anything" as totally normal. The location of pens and notepads, copier how-tos, and networked phone systems confuse everyone at first. Don't let those early days of being overwhelmed discourage you. You'll quickly figure out how things work and soon feel like a functioning part of the team.

Working as a Team

Understanding how women's ministry fits within the organization of the church helps women's leaders understand their teammates' expectations. Most churches have diagrams or charts showing how pastors, staff members, and ministries relate to one another, no matter how small or large the church. Ask if your church has one, and if they don't, ask if you can compile an informal one so you can see where women's ministry fits. The pastor's administrative assistant should be able to assist you. Ask your pastor or supervising minister to show you how women's ministry fits in the schematic. Is it located under the umbrella of education or discipleship? The diagram might also show the structure of supervision among the church staff. Many leaders in women's ministry report to the senior pastor, the senior associate pastor, or the education minister. Understanding how church staff and church members interrelate as they minister together will help you feel more confident in your new responsibilities. It'll also encourage you to resource all areas of the church rather than develop an isolated area of ministry.

Building healthy networking skills with your co-workers will strengthen your ministry and create harmony in the workplace. Communicate the goals of women's ministry from the very beginning. Let your co-workers know that women's ministry wants to equip women to serve in whatever capacity of the church body God leads them. Let each ministry area know you are not there to recruit their volunteers to work in your area but, rather, to equip and minister to women so that they can serve out of their wholeness and fullness. I continue to repeat that premise over and over and consistently attempt to practice it.

Just today over lunch, a colleague discussed wanting to reach out to young moms and wondered if I considered it crossing into "my territory." I immediately responded, "What territory? Women's ministry is all about equipping women to serve wherever God calls them to serve in the church." Even though she'd heard me say it over and over, she still remembered the territorialism she'd seen in her previous church. Never tolerate that attitude in your leadership. The church is one body with many members, and Christ wants it to function that way. Be consistent in speech and in behavior. Women's ministry is there to strengthen the work of the church, and you're privileged to be a part of the process. Heed Paul's admonition in Ephesians 4:1–3, when he urges us to "live a life worthy of the calling you have received. Be completely humble and gentle; be patient, bearing with one another in love. Make every effort to keep the unity of the Spirit through the bond of peace."

Another way to strengthen relationships among staff members is to communicate the value women's ministry adds to the church as a whole. Check appendix 3 for the benefits of women's ministry, or you can compile your own personalized list. In what ways do you see the women's ministry contributing to the health of the church? Be ready to reference them at any time. Men respect this type of information, so be up front in sharing it.

Being Yourself

How often have you heard the phrase, "Just be yourself"? This same advice applies to your leadership responsibilities. You have nothing to prove. It's the call from God that qualifies you, so relax and enjoy the journey. Don't let insecurities tempt you toward a defensive attitude. Continue to ask for advice and directions as needed. Your transparency reminds others you're new and still learning the routines. They'll be quicker to assist and quicker to offer information. Men, and some women, tend to have a naturally competitive nature. Sometimes competition creates a playful atmosphere, but other times it interrupts the smooth working of the body of Christ. It's easy to understand if the number of people participating in your ministry area provides the only measure of a leader's success. Continue to remind yourself of your goals—equipping women to serve in whatever area of the church God leads them—and be the first to applaud and support successes in all areas of the church body. As ministry boundaries begin to blur, and as ministries begin to partner in their objectives, a whole new level of body life begins to emerge. Lead out in these styles of leadership. Model cooperation and support for other areas. You'll be amazed at the ways God will honor your efforts and at how quickly you'll become a part of the team.

Identifying Communication Styles

Discovering the unique way each of your co-workers communicates enhances the effectiveness of your own communication. It requires both observation and, sometimes, simply asking. Start with noticing how each communicates to you. Does he or she phone, email, or prefer to visit with you in person? That's the first clue. Second, pay attention to which forms of communication they respond to most consistently. I've found that some co-workers only respond to phone calls instead of emails or notes. I've learned to stop by in person with my question for some. Others prefer I leave a note in their box. They like a piece of paper where they can write out their response. If you find you have difficulty discovering someone's communication style, simply ask how they prefer you contact them. I'll always remember my surprise to learn our reserved minister of finance preferred us dropping by his office. He chose a personal visit over emails, paperwork, or phone calls. Discovering how to effectively communicate will make your administrative tasks so much easier, efficient, and enjoyable. Be sure to identify your own preferred style in the process and let others know the best way to contact you. You'll be better equipped to function as an efficient and effective team member, and amazed at the diversity you'll discover in the process.

Following Protocol

Church members often fail to realize the responsibilities of the weekday staff and employees. Even if there's only a pastor and part-time church secretary, they still must handle finances, records, and phone calls during the week. They have reports, deadlines, and other specific responsibilities. Anyone who lacks prior experience in the workplace might feel surprised and confused by the procedures, rules, and regulations. Room reservation and setup, childcare, cleanup, and lockup all require procedures if things are going to run smoothly. In addition, knowing backup procedures prevents delay when you discover the room you reserved is locked. Not following in-house procedures creates a ripple effect of frustration and inconvenience for everyone. Understanding and respecting protocol might feel daunting at times, but it will serve you well.

"Oops, I'm Sorry"

Your responsibilities have placed you into a new family with all the typical dynamics of family life. Stress, deadlines, and cramped workspaces all contribute to misunderstandings. The same things that create harmony within a home create harmony in the workplace. Everyone makes mistakes. There's no need to react defensively when you do. You'll make mistakes when you learn new tasks, and you'll also make mistakes when you take risks and try something new. Don't let a fear of slipups keep you from trying new things.

I often respond to corrections with, "Oops. I made a mistake." Friends and colleagues expect to see an "oops" on the subject line of my emails at least once a month! What do you do when the error was actually a lack of effective communication from someone else to you? Just say you misunderstood the communication, and you'll be glad to correct the situation. Pointing fingers and arguing create negative feelings and build resentment. Focus on accomplishing the goal rather than on who made the mistake. Correct the mistake, apologize if that's appropriate, regroup, and move forward.

Offering Encouragement

Learn to be an encourager. Share those wonderful thoughts you have of others with them. When was the last time the praise team blessed you by one of their songs? When was the last time you told them or their leader? Whose laughter or consistent welcoming smile brightens your day? Whose wise counsel do you seek? Write notes or emails, or drop by their office and share your appreciation. My husband manages a Christian radio station and cites some pretty interesting statistics. Every response they receive from a listener by letter, email, or phone represents five hundred listeners who intended to respond but never got around to it! I'd love to have that same kind of data on face-to-face encouraging words. Expressing appreciation contributes to a song in the heart and a spring in the step of others. Let's not be one of the five hundred but be the one who actually takes the time to share.

Encouragement comes in other ways. Co-workers have personal struggles and daily challenges in their responsibilities just like you. Some jobs fall in the category of "thankless." I recently had the opportunity to hear a speaker addressing teamwork ask, "What is the name of the person who empties your trash can every day or wipes down the break table?" She broke the long silence by explaining the importance of every team member and how acknowledging their contribution strengthens the team. The more time you spend on the church campus, the more you'll see how effective affirmations create a positive environment. Be known as an encourager who assists the body in accomplishing God's work by keeping the working components well lubricated with thoughtfulness.

Setting Healthy Boundaries

Learning to put a healthy boundary in place between your women's ministry responsibilities and your home life takes time. I regularly seek my husband's objectivity on certain issues, but I'm careful to evaluate what's healthy to talk about and what's not. Too many negative conversations can bring a black cloud into our home. Perhaps you can recall hearing stories about your husband's or close friend's work. You want to understand the big picture, but you don't want the emotional clutter of details. You want to pray about the big decisions and responsibilities together without getting bogged down in gossip. After lots of trial and error, I feel Gary and I have found what works well for us, and I'm confident you will work your own way through to a healthy boundary in your home. If you're single, you'll want to pay attention to those same guidelines as you talk with friends about staff dynamics. Church staff members have human frailties just like everyone else. We're responsible for praying for them, not talking about them.

So, how do you cope with the stress of leadership if you don't dump it all at home? I typically "spread it around." That doesn't mean I dump it on everybody and anybody, but rather, I carefully consider which person can provide a healthy sounding board for what I'm dealing with. Perhaps it is a member of the leadership team, a girlfriend, a church staff member, or even a Christian counselor. God will guide you as you develop strategies for establishing healthy boundaries and for coping with stress.

Sharing the "Pie"

Working with the blessings and limitations of church budgets consumes a large portion of leadership discipline and creativity. Budgets also create a potential point of territorialism and conflict because there's only so much to go around. I've heard people say, "God owns the cattle on a thousand hills" and to "dream big." But day-to-day management also means working responsibly with what God has provided. Most women's ministries work on shoestring budgets. They work to cover the cost of events with registration fees. Individual women often absorb expenses and never ask for reimbursement for items like name tags, desserts, snacks, or flower arrangements. Their willingness to give is a great blessing, but as the ministry grows, so will the financial needs. I mentioned previously that church leadership knows ministry costs money. Part of your leadership responsibilities demand you look for ways to effectively communicate these growing needs. This is also an opportunity to incorporate your negotiating skills. Ask specifically for what you need. Then be ready to negotiate until you find a workable plan for moving forward—either now or at a future date. The simple strategy of negotiation means, if plan A isn't feasible, what about plan B? Plan C is asking, "May I return to discuss plan A in six months?"

Ask when the budget planning period occurs and when the deadline is for submitting budget requests. I discovered the benefits of asking for the definition of a "reasonable budget request" as we planned for the expense of leadership development. This would be a new budget item that might draw extra scrutiny, and we wanted the request to be as feasible as possible. I investigated beforehand what the finance committee would consider an appropriate leadership development expense—attending a conference, subscribing to a magazine, bringing in a trainer, purchasing a video-driven study, or financing a teaching/equipping retreat. The committee eventually approved our request to bring in a trainer. Once our budget line item was established, we've been able to annually offer a variety of training options.

In addition to reasonable requests, discover if existing church accounts might cover some of the ministry's needs. We needed lightweight tables for our small group studies and discovered this particular expense qualified for a capital account expense for items used by multiple ministry areas. Perhaps media or technology accounts could help with a new TV/DVD player for your women's Bible studies. If you discover a training opportunity you'd like to attend, ask about accounts that might supplement transportation expenses or registration fees. Be sure to budget for these expenses next year. Start small and then increase as the needs increase. Remember that as the church and staff see the benefits of a vibrant women's ministry, they'll respond supportively. Your budget will grow as God blesses and strengthens his church one woman at a time.

For Reflection

1. Joining the church staff as a volunteer, part-time worker, or full-time worker launches a wonderful new season of personal growth. What area of growth are you particularly excited about?

2. Understanding how women's ministry fits within the organization of the church helps women's leaders understand their teammates' expectations. How is your church's leadership organized? Sketch it out on a piece of paper. In what areas do you need more information?

3. Sometimes women feel they must prove themselves. When was the last time you let insecurities tempt you toward a defensive attitude?

4. Leadership responsibilities also bring opportunities for stress. Everyone makes mistakes. How do you respond when you make a mistake?

9

CONNECTING THROUGH WOMEN'S MINISTRY

Now the body is not made up of one part but of many.

1 Corinthians 12:14

During the formative stages of her church's women's ministry, Doris saw a need for women to know about opportunities for ministry already in place. First, she began writing down activities she knew about. Then she started asking others, including the pastor's assistant, church receptionist, and individual Sunday morning Bible study classes. She discovered far more ministries than she initially anticipated. Next, she thought through how to make this list available to current and new church members. This initial inventory provided a foundation for growing their women's ministry because of the entry points it offered women to connect with the body of Christ.

I t's been challenging to find a descriptive word for how women's ministry fits within the structure of the local church. We could describe women's ministry as an *in-frastructure*, but the word needs a little softer feel. By combining the idea of infrastructure with a woman-friendly gardening concept, we arrive at a terrific word—*trellis*! The lengthwise poles of a trellis provide invaluable support, but the crossbars create a gridlike pattern representing another key component of Women's Ministry—networking. That's exactly what Doris did when she organized the ministries in her church. See if this summary statement helps you understand a little better the work of women's ministry and how it fits within the local church: *Women's ministry provides a trellis-shaped infrastructure offering support and networking opportunities for women to grow and produce fruit as they discern God's call upon their lives.* Let's take a closer look at the concept of networking.

Networking 101

Women tend to respond to needs around them and often take action with little or no prompting. When they respond to the same type of need over and over, a ministry begins. I remember when Doris discovered a little-known ministry through Arlene, the pastor's assistant. Arlene used these women on a regular basis, but no one else seemed to know about what they did. When someone died without a small group Bible study or friends to provide a family meal the day of the funeral, Arlene phoned Laverne. Laverne in turn contacted women from her volunteer list to help with a meal. Arlene only had to make one phone call to meet this family's needs. The ministry had no name, so Doris named it the Bereavement Meals Ministry and added it to her growing list. This same pattern of meeting needs happens again and again throughout the local church. Networking provides a clearinghouse for current activities in the church as well as new opportunities for discipleship and service as they develop.

Doris continued to discover a wide variety of outreaches. Peggy drove with four other women to a state hospital specializing in pulmonary diseases where patients often stayed for weeks or months far away from friends and family. These ladies visited one morning a week, bringing magazines, cards, smiles, and prayers for the residents. Now they had a way to let others know about the outreach. Ann met monthly with friends to write personal notes welcoming city newcomers or notes of solace to those experiencing personal losses. Just like the hospital visitation team, they rejoiced that other women would learn of their group and possibly join them. Doris kept her list updated, and the women's leader not only publicized it but also referenced it when women inquired about opportunities for service. Networking these ministry points strengthened the body of Christ by helping others discover ways to meet needs.

Reaching Women on the Fringes

Our pastor loves to announce the church membership count and then add the disclaimer, "Only the FBI could find one-third of them!" Every church body grieves over members who actively served at one time but have slowly drifted away. I've seen it recently in my peer group. Couples sometimes lose their connections to the church when they no longer have children involved in youth activities. These empty nesters often spend weekends visiting their college-aged kids or traveling to visit grandchildren. Their attendance becomes more and more sporadic until one day they're officially "missing." Women's ministry offers an excellent resource to draw them back into the church. These women possess a rich variety of life experiences and leadership abilities. Track them down! Networking them with opportunities and needs at the church provides a fresh new challenge. It also puts them on teams with younger women where valuable mentoring occurs.

Reserved or shy women comprise another group on the fringes. Women's ministry creates a rich environment for them to flourish. Women who feel most comfortable on the outskirts often feel cautious and inadequate to lead. They make excellent leaders, though, because they've served behind the scenes observing leaders for years. Drawing them into leadership or co-leadership gives them an opportunity to discover their strengths. Don't wait for them to volunteer. Offer a personal invitation. They have so much to offer!

Getting the Word Out

Just a few years ago, women contacted one another from the limits of their kitchens, wandering only as far as the length of their phone cord. They redialed until they reached their friend Betty, Sue, or Alice. Today women use their pre-programmed cell phones to call or text message one another while they run errands. Caller IDs on their home answering machines screen callers, sort messages into family members' voice mail folders, or forward messages to cell phones. Women also touch base through email and instant messaging. Bluetooth allows hands-free communication, and a BlackBerry provides a virtual office anywhere you travel. Just imagine what the future holds! As you look for ways to notify women of opportunities for spiritual growth, use systems already in place like church newsletters and weekly worship folders. Include information in small group announcements and email groups. Some opportunities might qualify for a general church announcement at the end or beginning of the worship service or on image magnification screens.

Getting Past a Woman's Filters

Finding a way past a busy woman's mental screening poses a huge challenge. We've all developed the ability to screen out the constant bombardment of information and to selectively attend to only what interests us. Unfortunately, this same mental screening makes getting a woman's attention quite complex. Consider yourself a reference point for the high volume of information a woman screens or processes each day. Think about what gets your attention and what form of information you find most useful. I use the windowsill above my sink for things needing immediate attention, like invitations or dental appointments. I prefer receiving just the facts, clearly printed in large type on a postcard. I don't like searching through paragraphs of information for the time, date, and location. I also prefer email rather than a phone call. But an email followed up by a phone call works even better. Just working through the complexities of my own world offers me insight for navigating the informational challenges of other women's lives.

Regardless of today's diverse forms of communication, personal invitations remain the most effective avenue of reaching women and getting past their filters. By including in the publicity the phrase "bring a friend" or "guests eat free," you're encouraging women to invite other women. You can also offer an information table at gatherings to provide that personal contact women appreciate. Make it eye-catching, though. I'll always remember the first time we set up a Bible study registration table in our new foyer. We stood there with welcoming smiles, but women just returned our smiles and walked on past. We needed something visible above the crowd that would draw them over to us. We traded our beige tablecloth for a lime green and pink polka-dot shower curtain. We placed a colorful sign on a tall easel on top of the table. We added a tall pink and lime green flower arrangement for the final touch. The following Sunday women walked straight through the crowd to stop by the table! That got their attention. We broke through their filters.

Walk through the back rows of the worship center any Sunday morning and notice those sitting there or near the exits. You'll probably find some of the "fringe" women we mentioned earlier. Smile, speak, and extend a personal invitation to an event or small group Bible study. You'll be surprised to discover how many will come because you took time to personally invite them and answer their questions. In addition to personal invitations, continue your quest to discover a wide variety of formats for your information, including using special events for effective communication opportunities. Even in this setting, getting their attention still requires creativity. Consider using a combination of handouts, skits, and announcements for upcoming opportunities.

Brochures and Flyers

Brochures provide an ongoing overview of your ministry. You can print them annually with key dates for upcoming events, then keep them available for visitors and new members. We plan our new brochure in June, print it in July, and mail it in August. The back panel includes the fall discipleship and event opportunities. We print twice as many brochures as we need and leave the back panel blank for a second mailing in the spring. Consider cost-effective options. You can print attractive brochures on your home computer for the cost of paper and ink cartridges. You can use colorful-brochure-formatted paper or print them in full color at the printers. Simply make your decision based on your printing budget and the target group.

I visited recently with two women working alongside their husbands in church planting at a resort community in Idaho. They told me their posters and brochures took top priority because they had to stand out among all the glitzy notices distributed in that elite community. They understood the priority of catching a woman's attention and spent a large percentage of their meager budget on printing based on their target group.

Consider supplementing general information brochures with flyers that include more detailed information about the studies or upcoming events. Flyers offer flexibility that allows you to change and update them as needed. I like to purchase packages of colorful bordered paper. Even though it adds to the cost, it's worth the investment. We've noticed women will pause and pick it up if it's attractive and colorful. You also can mail or email flyers, distribute them in Sunday morning small groups, and keep a supply available at the information center or women's table. They're also convenient for women to pick up several and take to work for their colleagues and friends. You can post this same information on a website.

Websites, Radio, Newspapers, and Television

Many churches have a website ranging from basic to elaborate, depending on the needs of the members. A growing percentage of women prefer the convenience of visiting a website for the information they need rather than receiving printed information. Investigate your options for networking women's information on your church's website. Many allow browsers to click on individual ministry areas and see information specific to those areas. A website also has the potential to provide additional services, like purchasing event tickets or making childcare registrations. Seek out a woman with website skills who would like to assist you in investigating these options. It just might be the place of service she's been looking for in the body of Christ.

Women are increasingly using the Internet for connecting for prayer and ministry. An eleven-week-old infant recently underwent open-heart surgery in Houston, 150 miles from friends and family. A blog provided updates during the surgery and afterward during the critical recovery period. Family members and friends could pray through each new development and post encouraging messages. Jennifer Kennedy Dean created a blog to keep family members abreast of her husband's recently diagnosed brain tumor. Women who had participated in Jennifer's Bible studies and conferences on prayer began logging on and prayerfully sharing in her family's journey. I consider reading Jennifer's daily postings one

100

of the most intimate and moving experiences of my spiritual journey. I watched Jennifer live out her faith during the last six weeks they shared as husband and wife. We couldn't have even imagined this type of communication five years ago.

Podcasts will soon be another common form of networking information as women download sermons and other forms of spiritual enrichment from the Internet to their iPods. Women will no longer be limited by their physical location. They'll enjoy the benefits of both flexibility and mobility as they explore new ways to connect with their sisters in Christ.

Public service announcements on radio and television offer another option for networking information. Perhaps you have a Christian radio station in your area. They typically have a community bulletin board featuring local Christian activities. You can often check their websites to find guidelines for submitting your information. Cable companies often have a local events channel, and some television stations offer a community bulletin board segment with their newscasts. Evaluate the expense and effectiveness of newspaper ads, both printed and online versions. Also investigate options for submitting information to their community calendar. Find out the categories of events and formats for the information, along with deadlines for submission. If all this sounds tedious to you, consider delegating these responsibilities to someone who enjoys details. You just might discover one of those shy women who enjoys keeping up with these types of ministry needs.

As you constantly contend with our world's information overload, you'll discover the rhythm of the relationship between the recipient and the sender. Just today I read an interview with Shaun Winn, marketing director of a Christian youth ministry specializing in events. He gives this advice:

> One of the biggest things to remember is not to assume anything. Don't assume people will understand the Christian-ese that makes up the wording of your communication. . . .

101

Don't assume they will read the advertisements you print in the newspaper, or hear the radio ads you buy or the church bulletins you get space in. Don't assume they will understand the heart of what you're doing or your intent. Always be thinking how people might miss your promotions and the alternatives you can use to reach as many people as you can using as many tools as you can to draw them in.[1]

Until a future development rescues us from the challenges of reaching women with information, it will continue to be a changing and demanding part of leadership. Let's never give up looking for creative and effective ways to reach women with the Good News and the good things available through women's ministry.

For Reflection

1. The word *trellis* describes very well how women's ministry functions in the overall organizational structure of the church. How do you describe the function of a trellis? How do you see it relating to women's ministry?

2. Women's ministry is an excellent resource to draw women on the fringes back into the actively functioning church body. What ways do you plan on networking them with opportunities and needs at the church?

3. Getting past a busy woman's mental screening devices with opportunities for involvement is a common challenge. What are your top two favorite formats for receiving publicity about church opportunities?

4. Leaders can never give up looking for creative and effective ways to reach women with information about women's ministry. Name four ways you plan on communicating with the women in your church.

10

REACHING INWARD
THROUGH MEETING NEEDS

When my spirit grows faint within me,
it is you who know my way.

Psalm 142:3

BOBBIE BURKS

Bobbie Burks enjoyed working with the youth in her church. Her spontaneous laughter and quick wit naturally drew young people to her unconditional loving nature. During a career change, Bobbie felt the stirring of a longtime desire to counsel, so she set out by faith to acquire the necessary credentials. During the following years, she counseled as a volunteer and as a private practitioner. Now she serves as part of a church counseling staff. Many of the women she sees come as referrals through the women's ministry. Just like the youth, women easily respond to her humor, unconditional love, and biblical perspectives. She followed the Holy Spirit's prompting in her life and now provides a rich resource for Christian women in her church and community.

George Barna's research shows the local church moving toward a crisis. As far back as 1991, his research indicates a 22 percent drop in women's church attendance and a 21 percent drop in the percentage of women volunteering at church.[1] His research team also discovered that women tended to stop attending church when they face burnout rather than decline requests to serve. He concluded that churches needed to move beyond just accessing women as a large volunteer base to also considering ways to minister to them. Barna's research influenced our church leadership to reach inward and explore ways to address personal needs of the women in our church.

As God begins to reveal women's needs in your church, you'll discover ministry areas as diverse as the women in your church. Even though you might feel overwhelmed or weighed down by them, don't panic! You're not the one responsible for meeting them. The body of Christ is. God has placed you in a unique place as a leader to both encourage and to assist women in ministering to one another.

Women often seek spiritual guidance from friends or another woman before they seek it from the church pastoral staff. Having a female contact on the church staff in either a volunteer or paid position facilitates this initial connection. Before a woman will reach out for help, she must perceive a nonjudgmental atmosphere where she feels safe to communicate her needs. Women in leadership can learn how to create this emotionally safe environment where women feel they can come with their hurts and needs.

Addressing a Diversity of Needs

Women struggle with a wide assortment of needs that vary according to the season of life: sexual purity challenges; anxieties of career choices; newlywed concerns; young mom, working mom, and single mom exhaustion; crisis of divorce; concerns of maturing single women who've never been married; anxieties of rebellious adolescents; caregivers' fatigue; menopausal issues; disorientation from an empty nest; options of retirement; grief of widowhood; assisted living challenges; and the isolation of nursing home or homebound living.

When the diversity of needs feels overwhelming, look for women God has placed within the church or within the

105

church community at large with a similar life experience. These women can come alongside other hurting women and express the compassion of Jesus Christ.

My first encounter with this pairing of life events began with a simple conversation. One woman shared the healing influence of a Bible study on abortion. She'd experienced a medically terminated pregnancy at her doctor's recommendation many years before women understood the emotional and spiritual ramifications. She wanted me to know about the study. She also wanted to make herself available to share the healing she'd found with any other woman desiring companionship on her own healing journey. Within a month, a vibrant elderly woman came into my office to share a lifelong hurt from the days of being a war bride. She and her husband shared only a few days as newlyweds before the war separated them, but conception occurred. Due to the high risk of death in her husband's assignment, he responded to her notification with a simple "Take care of it." She felt the responsibility of submission and terminated the pregnancy. She'd carried the pain with her into her senior years and wanted release. How blessed I felt to have the former lady as a resource so they could share the journey together. Several months later that same senior adult woman bounced into my office wearing a radiant smile. She felt forgiven and free to leave her pain with the Lord—all because another woman walked with her through her grief. I was sold on the power of pairing.

The Power of Pairing

From that earliest pairing experience, our women's leadership team began gathering information of other women's life experiences. We eventually came up with a listing we called "Life Experiences Inventory" (see appendix 5). We continue to ask women to read over the list and check experiences they're willing to use to encourage another woman. I keep the sheets in a confidential file folder and reference them as needed. Occasionally women come by and personally share their story. Because of confidentiality concerns, they prefer telling it rather than recording it on paper. Sheila West ministers to women at her church in The Villages in Florida. She has a group of story gatherers she calls the "story squad." These women consciously listen for women's stories God can use to encourage other women.

Paul reminds us of the goal of suffering in 2 Corinthians 1:3–4: "Praise be to the God and Father of our Lord Jesus Christ, the Father of compassion and the God of all comfort, who comforts us in all our troubles, so that we can comfort those in any trouble with the comfort we ourselves have received from God." Experiencing the Father of compassion and the God of all comfort in the midst of emotional pain gives meaning to suffering. God redeems the loss even further when we comfort others with the same comfort we received from God. Yet I'm constantly amazed at how few life experiences women willingly check on the inventory. I've realized too many women remain spiritually stuck in their own healing journey. I live with a passionate and ongoing prayer: I pray Christian women will not stop short; I pray they will seek to know God's tender mercies for themselves and then share them with their sisters in Christ. It's part of God's design for the body of Christ, and women's ministry provides an avenue to facilitate it.

Intentional Mentoring

Sandy, a single mom, seldom managed to stretch her food budget to the end of the month, so a friend offered to shop with her and point out cost-cutting tips. Spontaneous mentoring happens when women get together. It's also one of the many side benefits of small group Bible studies. Intentional mentoring carries an even greater impact because we also encourage one another in the area of sanctification, growing in Christlikeness. Women's ministry provides an excellent arena for organizing mentoring. If this is a direction you feel the Lord moving, begin praying for the woman God has in mind for leadership. Even though you'll want to support mentoring with your leadership, look for someone else to provide the logistical guidance.

As you and the mentoring ministry leader discover the dynamics of mentoring, you might also uncover some surprising trends. You might notice that those who enroll are either working women, single women, or women not already a part of a Sunday morning or weekday Bible study—women looking for a sense of connection that the mentoring ministry can provide. Other women might be seeking guidance in specific areas of their lives, like health issues. Pairing mentors and mentees for a determined time frame offers a powerful way to strengthen believers in their faith. If fewer mentors than mentees sign up, visit with the women you'd consider quality mentors and ask about their hesitations. Visiting with them about their concerns often calms their fears. Perhaps they're worried about time constraints, feelings of inadequacy, or even just the title of "mentor." Women in their midforties and above often view the younger generation as competent and self-sufficient. The college degrees, new homes, new cars, and technological skills communicate "everything is under control." You'll increase your mentor recruitment once you point out that the younger generation often struggles with financial, marriage, and parenting insecurities just like the generations before them. If you continue to have difficulty recruiting mentors, consider using a less intimidating word. We chose the name "Intentional Friends" as a way to bypass this issue.

Discovering expectations of each participant in the application process helps the commitment succeed. Providing a prayer support team that checks in and prays for each partnership also strengthens the mentoring relationship. You'll also want to consider the length of the mentoring relationship, application process, and pairing process. Programs like Woman2Woman[2] pair mentors and mentees according to spiritual age rather than chronological age. This works particularly well in a church with a large number of new believers. You can view mentoring ministry resources and sample forms in appendix 8.

Reaching Moms

Young mothers, whether at home or in the workplace, face very long days. They cope with interrupted sleep, endless clutter, and the insecurity of wondering if they're doing it all right. Women's ministry can make such a difference in a young mother's life simply by creating opportunities for them to be with other mothers. Consider implementing some of the organized programs for mothers like MOPS (Mothers of Preschoolers)[3] or Mom to Mom.[4] You can also create your own program based upon the specific needs of your moms. Young moms need spiritual nourishment, fellowship, and childcare. Scheduling your moms' group during your regular Bible study time allows them to fit into childcare arrangements you already have in place. It also brings them into the flow of seeing other age groups of women studying the Bible. This will help when they're ready to make the transition from the moms' group into a regular Bible study group.

Moms' groups can choose from a large selection of Scripture-based parenting studies.[5] Some moms groups alternate between parenting studies and a Bible study. Some groups like Moms in Touch[6] meet solely for the purpose of praying for their children. Some groups schedule chat time the first thirty minutes. This not only allows flexibility in arriving, but it also meets their need to spend time interacting casually with other mothers. Occasionally God calls out a young mom to lead her peers in the moms' study. Generally, though, a woman past the young-mom stage of life can add insight and personal experience to the questions that come up. She also has a more predictable schedule—no teething babies and colicky long nights for her. A moms' group offers a rewarding ministry opportunity for a woman looking for a nurturing, fun-loving, energy-filled group of women to lead.

Reaching Widows

Most of us think of widows as women who have shared a long and satisfying life with their mate. Not true! Think about the widows in your own church and take note of their ages. You'll possibly discover widows in their thirties, forties, and fifties. Many widows still work and some still have children at home. Widows also face unique needs as they transition into life as a single woman. They don't feel ready to be a part of the singles ministry just yet, and they feel awkward with their former couple friends. They need support as they build new friendships and establish new routines. Other widows can provide companionship, laughter, and hope. They need to know that intense grieving will gradually become less invasive. They need to know that the days ahead will slowly take shape as God guides them in charting a new life-course. Elaine Cook's painful memories of facing life as a young widow with three small children fueled her to reach out to organize Widow2Widow, a growing network of outreaches to widows through the local church. It also offers special widow conferences providing fun and informative breakout sessions. Look to see what resources are available in your community and church, then consider God's timing for reaching out both formally and informally to the widows in your church.

Coping with Chronic Pain

Have you noticed how women seem to slowly disappear from church involvement when they're coping with chronic pain? I'm amazed at how many women cope with the mysterious muscle aches and debilitating pain of fibromyalgia.[7] They never seem to know when they'll have a "good" day or a "bad" day, and they hesitate to accept responsibilities or make commitments. They simply slowly drift away from the mainstream of church activities. Any woman with chronic pain needs the compassion of another woman who truly understands her struggles.

I remember Marsha's and Judy's hesitancy to talk about their pain—mostly because no one seemed to understand. For months I encouraged them to get together for a visit. I didn't understand yet that planning ahead for that type of self-care was beyond their energy limits. I eventually invited both of them to meet me for coffee and pedicures. While they visited, I listened and marveled at the power of two Christian women to encourage and refresh one another. A casual conversation over coffee launched a networking of other women in the church. Every few months they got together informally for "lunch and laughter" at a local restaurant. Women recently diagnosed and struggling to reshape their lives especially benefit from visiting with those who have discovered new rhythm and new hope for a chronic situation. I'm currently praying for a lady who has a knowledgeable awareness and a God-given empathy to provide leadership for these women. I'd love to see personal notes as well as phone calls and prayer support. I'm just trusting God's timing!

Facing Divorce

Single women have shared with me the hurts and rejection they felt in their churches after their divorce. They mentioned the uneasiness married women seemed to have in their presence. At first they thought they imagined it but later noticed the distinct protectiveness married women had of their husbands. Yikes! This was hard for me to believe, but many single women have confirmed similar experiences. Women's ministry can intentionally offer a safe place for divorced women to face their hurts and begin the healing journey.

Many churches have implemented a divorce recovery study that allows women to begin the healing journey together. Divorce Care[8] allows women to think through different areas of their life impacted by the divorce as they share twelve weeks of one another's stories of disappointments, shattered dreams, and grief. Sharing the journey with other women helps to diffuse the isolation and despair. Someone else understands the shame and guilt that accompany many divorces. Newly divorced women also need a women's Sunday morning Bible study to attend until they're ready to integrate into a coed singles' program. Women's ministry can facilitate this time of healing and transition for women facing this life-altering experience.

Journeying through Grief

Living in a fallen world creates endless heartaches and disappointments. Few of us really understand the healing power grieving offers. Even fewer truly understand the actual grieving process. We typically associate grief with the death of a loved one. But any loss necessitates grief work: job loss, divorce, illness, a mastectomy, kids leaving home, bankruptcy, relocation, caregiving, loss of a pet, or birth of a child with a disability. God designed grieving as the way to heal and move forward with life. Women's ministry can guide women in knowing how to identify and grieve losses in their lives through offering a grief recovery study. Pray that God will lead you to a woman in your church who has a burden for this area of need. Investigate resources on the market and be alert for new ones as you continue to learn about emotional health and the healing power of tears.[9]

Giving Permission

Many of us opt to avoid the painful realities of domestic violence among Christian couples. The complexities and confusion of this devastating tragedy overwhelm us. Brenda Branson and Paula Silva bring clarity to the broad spectrum of this issue through their definition of *domestic violence* as "a repeated pattern of behavior used to gain power and control over another through the use of intimidation, emotional abuse, verbal abuse, physical assault, or sexual abuse."[10] They also note that "one in every four women in each church community is currently being abused by their partner, or has experienced abuse at some time in the past."[11]

I remember the discomfort I felt several years ago listening to a radio talk show guest cite similar statistics of domestic violence in Christian homes and the church's silence on this escalating issue. Fortunately a caller phoned in the question on my mind: "How can the church break its silence?" The guest said the pastor can give victims permission to seek help publicly through sermons and privately in counseling. The church can also provide educational resources for the victims. I knew immediately this was where women's ministry could make a difference. I asked God to direct me to cost-effective and useful information. Within months, my sister brought me a small paperback resource she'd seen at a conference.[12] One of the men's Sunday morning small groups underwrote the cost of purchasing twenty copies for the women's table, where they discreetly disappeared within three months. Over the past five years, we've purchased hundreds more of these resources that continue

113

to provide permission to seek help for church members or friends of members. For more economical resources, check with your area crisis center for domestic violence for excellent brochures, usually available at no cost.

Connecting

There's a desperate need for good information in many other areas of need, and women's ministry can serve as a center of distribution. Since we began making resources on domestic violence available, we've also seen an increasing number of women making first contact for assistance in the women's office. They had begun to perceive our office as a safe place to disclose their hurts and fears. Larry Crabb calls the process *connecting*: "There is, obviously, a place for advice, insight, and friendly encouragement—but not at the center. I suggest that the absolute center of all powerful attempts to impact people for good is connecting."[13] Unconditional acceptance exists at the heart of connecting. He describes it this way:

> The truth of the Gospel and the presence of the Holy Spirit within us allows us to accept people for who they are, grieve over every failure to live out their true identity, and no matter what happens, continue to believe in what they could become—without demanding that it happen on our timetable or for our sakes or that we play a big part in making it happen.[14]

Treasure the quiet moments when women share their deepest hurts. Give them permission to share their tears. I've learned to move beyond my inner urge to calm and to distract them from their emotional pain. Instead, I share in their deepest hurt simply by waiting and being emotionally present. Larry Crabb believes in the healing power of tears shed in the presence of others. He says,

Most of our deepest tears are often shed alone. . . . But tears without an audience, without someone to hear and care, leave the wounds unhealed. When someone listens to our groanings and stays there, we feel something change inside us. Despair seems less necessary; hope begins to stir within.[15]

Continue to grow in your understanding of the struggles we face as humans in a fallen world. As social issues continue to grow more complex, we must continue to acquire new skills in meeting needs. Christian bookstores offer excellent books on lay counseling. Providing training for the women in your church will equip them to offer wise counsel informally for their friends and family members. They'll also be available to Christian sisters in need within the church. I've enjoyed membership in the American Association of Christian Counselors (AACC)[16] as one source of information relevant to women's issues.

Confronting Depression

A recent AACC magazine reports: "Women are three times as likely as men to be impacted by major depression and dysthymia, starting in adolescence and peaking between the ages of twenty-five and forty-five, during the childbearing years. . . . With every generation onset is becoming younger and risk factors higher."[17] Because of a personal experience with depression, I'm sensitive to symptoms in women and have a desire to make sure they have good solid information. Women's ministry provides an excellent opportunity for addressing that need. Several years ago, a friend provided me with a copy of a panel discussion on women and depression offered by the women's ministry of a local church. The panel featured a gynecologist/obstetrician, psychologist, pediatrician, and Christian counselor. We received permission to reproduce the seminar and to make it available at our women's table—a central location where women can pick up any resource related to women's ministry. In the last four years, women have picked up hundreds of copies. It's one of our most popular resources. I've also recently discovered a small pamphlet[18] that helps women distinguish between the finer emotional shades of rejection, grief, and depression. It also includes a depression inventory with directions for interpreting the score. Remain alert for new information you can make available to women. Also consider including a line item for educational or emotional health as you begin to build a budget. By offering a series of Bible studies that address emotional concerns of women—depression, codependency, forgiveness, grief, blended families, sexual abuse, etc.—women have an opportunity to apply biblical principles to their struggles.

Distorted Sexuality

I remember hearing the phrase "Friends' Generation" several years ago to describe the generation of young people growing up watching the TV show *Friends*.[19] The popular show ran almost ten years and significantly influenced young people in their acceptance of cohabitation and premarital sex. These *Friends* Generation women are now attempting to build healthy marriages and homes in spite of their oversexualized and/or promiscuous pasts—and they're in crisis.

Shannon Ethridge addresses these issues in her bestselling book, *Every Woman's Battle*.[20] The challenge of sexual purity confronts the women of our churches, and women's ministry can lead out in addressing this need. Recently, a beautiful young wife stopped by to share her own pursuit of purity and her desire to invite other women to join her. I was thrilled! Together we examined possible options. Women's ministry helped her locate resources as she wrote a thirty-day online Bible study, which went live on our website in fall of 2007 (www.gabc.org). We encourage the women who complete the online study to consider participating in a six-week accountability group of three women. We have no idea how God will use this, but we continue to move forward, prayerfully seeking God's leading and God's glory each step of the way.

In addition to oversexualization, women now face the confusion of sexual identity and same-gender attraction. The church struggles with knowing how to approach these difficult issues. Women's ministry needs to be a safe place for women to ask questions and find answers and resources. We must learn how to love as Christ loved and help bring these women into a comforting, healing relationship with him. God has begun to work through Christian organizations that can assist us, like Living Hope[21] and Exodus International,[22] as well as Focus on the Family's Love Won Out[23] conferences. Ann Paulk, a former lesbian, has written a helpful resource called *Restoring Sexual Identity: Hope for Women Who Struggle with Same-Sex Attraction.*[24] She says our support of those struggling with sexual identity is important because women

> making the unpopular decision to leave the homosexual life often find a great deal of opposition and very little encouragement. Some women must leave behind a way of life that has seemed inescapable and a community of like-minded women who represented their entire support system.[25]

When God brings these hurting women into your world, don't hesitate to express God's love, grace, and power for their needs.

Identifying Community Resources

Learn how to identify community resources for women as you become aware of their needs. Generally, some agency

117

will provide a complete updated listing. United Way organizes our local information, but it might vary from town to town. God will direct your path as you seek out community options through the local Crisis Shelter, Salvation Army, and government-assisted housing. Because our city is the medical hub for six counties, we often have wives or husbands needing housing during their loved ones' extended stay in the hospital. Establish a community bulletin board where notices can match needs with opportunities. Keep a record of individuals who rent rooms or are willing to take in someone for a limited time.

Assisting with Relocation

Susan Wells lived in her new town four lonely years before feeling like a part of the community. She remembered the loneliness so well that she began to look for ways to welcome newcomers to the area. She asked if women's ministry could assist her with this outreach. Susan addressed invitations to women with new gas and water connections and to new church members. A lively group of women arrived with umbrellas and wet shoes for the "Newcomer Coffee." They felt so desperate for new friends that unexpected spring showers and brisk winds couldn't keep them away! Susan discussed chapters from the book *After the Boxes Are Unpacked*[26] with her "new" friends for six weeks. Susan continues to offer a Newcomer Coffee each year. The eagerness in the eyes of the women who attend affirms their appreciation for the welcoming hug and the friendship Susan offers.

Single Moms

Our hearts ache watching the American family unravel. Single moms struggle with responsibilities of daily deci-

118

sions of parenting, custody challenges, financial shortages, loneliness, and insecurities. Imagine the difference when women's ministry can coordinate opportunities for support, fellowship, and parenting skills. Knowing they're not alone in the journey undergirds the women as they begin the process of rebuilding their lives.

Single moms comprise one of the largest groups of low-income families in our country. I overheard the singles' minister recently discuss a request for a single moms' food pantry, and I agreed with him—we didn't need one. No single in our church ever went hungry! Imagine my dismay the day a single mom dropped by for permission to visit the food pantry. I was the only one around, so we went together. I ached for her as she looked among the economy bags of rice and pinto beans for items her young children could take to school for lunch. I've become painfully aware that many single moms run short near the end of the month, especially if they've had unexpected car repairs or medical bills. One of the women's Sunday morning classes now assists with keeping the pantry stocked with nutritious and child-friendly foods.

Addressing Issues of Aging

One morning, I entered the building where I have an office and heard an amazing chorus of voices. It drew me down the hallways to a doorway where I could see a literal sea of gray. I stood there transfixed as I witnessed this portion of the body of Christ worshiping together, sharing the joys and challenges of their senior years. Women often face loneliness as they move into the early retirement years and beyond. Personal health issues, caregiving, and often widowhood accompany this season. Women's ministry can offer safe places to find information, support, and prayer. Hospital visitation/prayer ministry, shut-in ministries, retirement center Bible studies, and quilting ministries are just a few options

119

available to reach out with God's tender touch to the aging Christian woman. During recent years, I've watched some of our key women leaders move into retirement communities and begin small group Bible studies with their new friends. Many of the women who attend have never studied the Bible before. God's opening up an amazing new mission field to those available to serve him!

Supporting Needs of Mental Illness

The body of Christ continues to grow in its understanding of mental illness and in knowing how to offer support to family members. Ann's son first exhibited symptoms of schizophrenia during his junior year of college. Christian brothers and sisters who believed a lack of faith prevented God from healing him caused much heartache and confusion. Today Ann receives ongoing prayer support and encouragement from the women God has placed in her life through her local church. Even though each day brings new challenges, she knows she's not alone.

Janet called the women's ministry office when her own pain became too great to carry alone. She contacted women she knew who also struggled with children with mental illnesses and invited them to an evening of coffee and conversation. She asked Ann to direct their time together and ease the anxiety level among the women. I'll never forget the story of one of the women who attended. She said, "All I could do was cry when it was my turn to share. In fact, I cried all the way home. The tears, though, resulted from relief and joy of answered prayer. I'd prayed for eighteen months to find just one Christian woman who understood. When I walked into the room and saw all the other women, I realized God had abundantly answered my prayer. Now, whenever I cross paths with one of the women, we just embrace and our loneliness in the journey seems to vanish."

Email Networking

One effective strategy for meeting needs actually developed out of an act of desperation! Multiple needs converged one morning in the women's ministry office and I just felt overwhelmed. I knew lots of women who might want to help, but I didn't have time to contact all of them. I decided to compose an email stating the various needs. I then went through my address book and sent it to every woman I thought would want to know. By the end of the day, four women had met all the needs! As a result, we now have a Ministry in Motion E-Group.[27] Just today I received a request from a mother who works on Sunday and would like her five-year-old to get a ride to church. She lives outside of town. I sent out a Ministry in Motion email, and within thirty minutes, Kathy responded with, "I've forwarded this request to Trisha. She lives in that area and also teaches in the children's area. I just know she'll want to help meet this need!" Women's ministry has limitless opportunities to impact hurting women through networking resources available in the body of Christ. What a privilege to express Christ's own tender hands and gentle heart to one another!

For Reflection

1. When you begin to feel overwhelmed by the needs among the women of your church, look for women with a similar life experience who can step in for you. How has God used someone in your own life to encourage you during a difficult time?

2. Women mentor spontaneously and intentionally. Who would you consider a spiritual mentor in your life? How did the relationship develop?

3. Young moms need spiritual nourishment, fellowship, and childcare. What opportunities do the young moms have for Bible study at your church? What would you like to see happen in the future?

4. Treasure the quiet moments when women share their deepest hurts. How do you typically respond when another woman weeps in your presence? What skills would you like to develop in the area of offering a compassionate, listening ear?

PART III

ENJOYING FRUITFUL
LEADERSHIP

As the momentum of women's ministry begins to grow, you'll discover a deep desire to nurture growth in those you lead. You'll also want to sustain the excitement and anticipation of God at work. You'll feel the need to seek out ways to invest in leadership development of these women as well as identify additional leaders in each generation of women.

11

NURTURING SPIRITUAL GROWTH

David shepherded them with integrity of heart;
with skillful hands he led them.

Psalm 78:72

NANCY PAUL

Nancy and her husband, Alan, relocated his medical practice from Toronto to the Wild West—Texas! They expected to find cactus and longhorn cattle. Instead, they found pine trees and mourning doves, as well as Christ as their Savior. They hungered to grow and study God's Word. Nancy eventually joined the women's Bible studies, and when the coordinator for the studies moved away, Nancy volunteered. She loved to evaluate new studies and offered gifted coordination of each semester's selections. She regularly asked for an evaluation from each participant so she could make needed adjustments in the next session. She helped decide how many workbooks to purchase and coordinated small group facilitators. Today she continues to seek out equipping opportunities for those who lead. She's the women's director's right-hand woman in discipleship responsibilities. In addition, God recently opened opportunities for her to serve as the liaison between her local women's ministry and a new church work in her hometown, Toronto. She finds great pleasure in seeing her spiritual journey come full circle.

Remember the garden trellis analogy from chapter 9? Just as it works well for illustrating networking, it also effectively illustrates the concept of nurturing spiritual growth through women's ministry. I like to contrast the function of a flowerpot to the role of a trellis for a plant's growth. One *contains* the plant, the other *supports* the plant. Previous generations of leadership for women flourished using the container format. As time passed, though, culture changed and the container format began requiring high levels of maintenance. It lost the flexibility the next generation required. Women are asking for trellis-like support for spiritual growth and vitality. These components require a healthy balance between Bible study and ministry as well as a supple response to ongoing events within the world around them. The trellis concept also adjusts to women's mobility and the changing seasons of their lives. As my clematis vine rambled upward on its support this spring, I thought of the random movement of spiritual growth in each of our lives. Consistent spiritual leadership for women begins to produce this evidence of spiritual growth in a wide variety of areas. The desire for accountability offers one evidence of growth.

Seeking Accountability

Seeking accountability in our spiritual journey provides an essential component in leadership. Your leadership team and church staff provide two personal accountability resources. Seeking woman-to-woman accountability in a personal area of struggle—like overeating, overspending, inconsistent quiet time—makes us more accountable to God. Christ-centered recovery programs and other twelve-step programs have built-in systems for accountability through sponsorship, mentoring, and small groups. I want to discuss a different type of accountability many Western Christians avoid—accountability for what God has entrusted to us. Perhaps you're more familiar with the word *stewardship*.

Several years ago, I had the privilege of serving as part of a ministry team in Cuba. Last-minute government decisions sent us scurrying to random destinations rather than to our preplanned locations. I arrived at the home of a surprised pastor and his wife who expected a bilingual male. We quickly sent for an interpreter, and I prayed to discover what God had in store. I soon noticed the pastor's wife told the same story over and over through the interpreter: "I was sick for a long time, then I had a hysterectomy, and now they say I am well." I learned she had stopped teaching Bible studies on Sunday mornings and girls' groups on Sunday evening. She also no longer cooked or cleaned for her family. The female interpreter and I wondered if we were observing symptoms of depression and menopause. After I explained both conditions, her eyes lit up and she said, "I thought I was dying and no one would tell me!" Understanding her symptoms and hearing that she'd gradually begin to feel better provided the hope she needed.

I remember complaining to the Lord on the return flight. "Eunice's world is so hard. It's just not fair for me to have so many resources for serving you and for Eunice to have so few! I have shelves of Bibles, Bible studies, and resource books. I have paper in all shapes and colors and photo copiers for duplicating. She has no pencil or paper or resources to prepare her teaching, only a trickle of water in her shower, and not even an aspirin in her home—so many responsibilities as a pastor's wife and so few resources!" As I gently wept in my dismay, I remembered the biblical admonition, "From everyone who has been given much, much will be demanded; and from the one who has been entrusted with much, much more will be asked" (Luke 12:48). I reflected on this thought, then envisioned myself standing before the Lord, giving account of all my resources. I had a new complaint. "That's not fair either!" I wailed. "I didn't choose to be born in a country with religious freedom, educational opportunities, and an abundance of resources for ministry. I don't want to be accountable for all these!" I sat in stunned silence the rest of the flight.

That experience became a turning point in my leadership. I returned home and took inventory of unused opportunities to reach and equip women. I took a deep breath, prayed for direction and courage, and began exploring new ways to remain faithful. Howard Hendricks, a professor at Dallas Theological Seminary, spoke at our church the following summer and encouraged me further. He shared his burden and prayer for our congregation in his closing remarks. He said, "May you have faith and vision equal to your opportunities." I grabbed a pen and scribbled his words on the back of a pew envelope that now hangs prominently beside my computer. What a powerful prayer! I continue to pray it for myself, and now I pray it for you. We will all stand before a righteous God and give account of what he's entrusted to us. May God find in us a good and faithful servant.

Gathering for Bible Study

Small group Bible studies provide the foundation for women's ministry. Women have always naturally gathered with one another, just as Paul found Lydia and the other women at the riverbank worshiping on the Sabbath. The book *The Tending Instinct*[1] explains the biological benefits of women gathering, yet the information only validates what women already know. We just feel better when we get together!

One night when my husband returned from a long day at work, I remember listing all my woes as a mother of four preschool children. As he walked away, I heard him say, "What you need is a woman fix." I asked him what he meant, and he explained, "If I can get you with some women, you're good to go for at least six weeks." At the time I still didn't understand, but now I know exactly what he meant, and the research presented in *The Tending Instinct* verifies it. When the women gathered at the cross, they responded as God had designed them to respond. Recent research reveals that during stress, men and women both experience an initial rush of adrenalin. While men respond with a fight or flight, women experience a secondary chemical response of oxytocin. This hormone influences women to nurture and gather with one another. God designed within women a caring, or "tending and befriending," response as a way to cope with stress, and we see it in action at the cross.[2]

What a wonderful Creator to include in the complex design of women's bodies an innate response of nurturing and caring for one another! God designed women to feel better after they've been together. Combine "gathering" with Bible study and you have a wonderful combination. The challenge we face in the twenty-first-century church is creativity in scheduling opportunities for women to do just that. Considerations such as locations, times, childcare availability, and length and type of study challenge our planning abilities. Don't let these considerations daunt your enthusiasm. Through prayerful discernment and input from participants, you and your Bible study coordinator will make good decisions. All these options actually help us to address the diversified needs of today's woman. How blessed we are!

Hearing the Call to Prayer

Prayer undergirds all facets of women's ministry. It's also an area of misunderstanding and guilt. Most of us feel like we don't pray often enough or long enough. Friends email or phone asking for prayer. We promise to pray but then forget the promise. We know we need to pray for missionaries, the lost, our kids and husbands, family and friends, but we feel like we never quite measure up. I've been observing women who are growing in their prayer life and those who aren't growing. I've looked for threads of commonality in those responding to the call to pray. I've wondered, "Is this a calling from God or a gift from God to be able to pray in faith? Why do I see more senior adult women than younger women praying? Are those who pray women who have faced hardships in life and found strength at the throne of God? Has a history of answered prayer encouraged more prayer?"

I'll never forget visiting a retirement center for pastors and their wives in Cuba. After seeing such overwhelming deprivation in the country, I especially dreaded witnessing it among those precious saints. How wrong I was! I found the residents cheerfully rocking and visiting in the breezeways. I entered one sparsely furnished room to find a white-haired woman leaning over her open Bible. She looked up with a broad grin. After brief exchanges of Spanish greetings, I exhausted my conversational abilities, and she returned to her Bible reading and prayer. She still had work to do, and she took her responsibilities seriously as she influenced the world for Christ from her little room.

The work of prayer is a spiritual discipline that requires just that—discipline. It also reflects the sensitivity of the heart of the one praying. Those who lead women must ask how we can encourage and equip women to pray. Few contemporary authors and teachers have influenced my prayer life as much as Jennifer Kennedy Dean.[3] She has taught me the realities of how to "pray without ceasing." She calls it "living a praying life." Jennifer says,

> Prayer is not limited to a segment of our lives or to a scheduled event in our days. It is an attitude of receptivity in which we live every moment. It is being open to Him at all times. It is living in the presence of God, always in the process of being reshaped and recreated by Him.[4]

I've learned to begin silently praying as soon as someone begins describing a prayer need. If appropriate, I ask if I can pray with her right then. I've also learned to be careful about what I promise. I commit to pray for others when the Lord brings them to my mind.

When the disciples asked Jesus to teach them to pray, Christ offered a model (see Matthew 6:9–13). He showed them how to pray to God as their Father. He acknowledged God as holy and requested God's kingdom and perfect will come into the circumstances of their lives. Jesus acknowledged that all physical needs are met by God and that through him we receive forgiveness for sins. Through prayer we acknowledge our need to forgive others and our need for protection from evil. When women discover the freedom of living within God's presence with a heart attitude reflected in Christ's model prayer, the floodgates of heaven will open and God will begin a mighty outpouring of his power among and through the women of your church. And it all begins with you. Ask Jesus to teach you how to live a praying life.

Equipping through Conferences

Hosting your own conference or attending area conferences for women provides an opportunity to learn, worship, develop friendships, and experience quality entertainment. Whether planning one or attending one, you'll want to evaluate the focus of the event and see if it's in line with your women's ministry's purpose statement and current spiritual needs. As we have more and more opportunities to attend Christian conferences and concerts, Eugene Peterson, translator of *The Message*, cautions us,

> A huge religious marketplace has been set up in North America to meet the needs and fantasies of people just like us. There are conferences and gatherings custom-designed to give us the lift we need. There are books, videos, and seminars that promise to let us in on the Christian "secret" of whatever we feel is lacking in our life—financial security, well-behaved children, weight loss, sex, travel to holy sites,

exciting worship, celebrity teachers. . . .We become consumers of packaged spiritualities.[5]

Dr. Peterson's strong statement will keep us focused on seeking God's leadership and discernment as we utilize conferences, retreats, and workshops in nurturing leadership.

Planning your first large event feels all-consuming and literally overwhelming to those of us without the gift of administration. I strongly suggest you find someone who does have those strengths if you don't. Angela Yee's resource, *The Christian Conference Planner*,[6] covers all aspects of planning, from "why have a conference?" to "wrapping up a conference." I suggest locating resources that can help you chart the process of praying, planning, and hosting the event. That way you'll feel more confidence in reaching the team's desired goals.

Responding to Our World

Nurturing spiritual growth in women requires walking with them through community and even world crisis. Eugene Peterson visited our community and participated in a brief question-and-answer session with our pastor. I'll always remember the twinkle in his eyes when he talked about the joy he'd had as a pastor. "There's such intimacy in relationships of those you lead. You share in their lives in such a tender way, their marriages, births of children, deaths, joys, and sorrows. I wouldn't trade it for the world." As you build relationships with the women you lead, you'll also discover the intimacy of sharing the journey with them. You'll cry together and celebrate together. Place the needs of those you lead first, and they'll grow in trust of you as their leader. People are always more important than programs or schedules. Allow for flexibility as life intervenes. Offer grace when someone calls and needs to be replaced in a leadership position because she's unexpectedly become a caregiver to one of her parents. Encourage her in her new God-given assignment and assure her that God will provide someone to assume her responsibilities. Reassure her you'll be holding a place in ministry just for her when she's able to return. Let her know that you trust God's leadership in her life and that you'll be supporting her in prayer. Then trust God yourself to continue to meet leadership needs within your women's ministry.

Addressing the Seasons of Life

Because both of my parents struggled with finishing life strong, I've closely watched others to see how they complete their journeys. I've discovered in the process that we have lots of options in how we approach each season of our life. As a young mother, I felt like I'd always be overwhelmed by the tasks of parenting. I couldn't imagine the freedom of having an empty nest. I've watched those I lead pass through their own seasons of life, and I've sought to encourage them in each one. Each period of life directly impacts their ability to volunteer or lead in ministry—whether they're a new mom, a new employee, or a new widow. Just last week a friend shared her observation that women generally have three windows of personal time in their lives: before they have children, when the children leave home, and after retirement before becoming caregivers. Women spend most of those in-between years responding to the needs around them.

A young mom who'd enjoyed being active in women's ministry recently dropped by with her six-week-old daughter. As we visited, she asked, "How does a mother of three little ones find time for women's ministry?" I said, "A mother of three little ones has a full-time ministry! Your responsibilities are to care for them, nurture your relationship with your husband, and learn how to spiritually feed yourself in the process. This season won't last long. You'll eventually have snitches of time to do other things." I've learned that supporting women during each season of life nurtures their leadership skills as wives and mothers. One day, hopefully, they'll be visiting and encouraging other young moms with the same wise counsel.

Accepting Women's Mobility

My heart always sinks when a woman in leadership announces her husband's transfer to a new city. I inevitably feel abandoned and tempted to beg for her to stay. Only when you're sensitive to the Holy Spirit can you rejoice that her gifts and talents will soon be blessing another body of believers. In the meantime, she needs your encouragement that she'll survive the move. She also needs a sense of closure in her current responsibilities and in friendships she's leaving behind. It's all part of leading—investing, equipping, and sending off women to minister elsewhere. Paul had many goodbyes in his travels and often recorded his longings for fellow Christians in his letters. To the believers in Philippi he wrote, "God can testify how I long for all of you with the affection of Christ Jesus" (Phil. 1:8). He offers the elders of the church in Ephesus a special expression of grace: "Now I commit you to God and to the Word of his grace, which can build you up and give you an inheritance among all those who are sanctified." Paul then "knelt down with all of them and prayed. They all wept as they embraced him and kissed him. . . . Then they accompanied him to the ship" (Acts 20:32, 36–38).

I once had an opportunity to hear Dr. Jeanine Boseman[7] teach during an intensive two-and-a-half-day class on "The Relationships of Women." The last day of class she announced,

> Life is a series of hellos and goodbyes. We must learn well how to say both. Today we'll say our goodbyes. Many of us will not

see one another again until heaven. Is there anything you might have thought about saying to another student but haven't? If so, we're going to take five minutes for you to share your thoughts and to say your goodbyes. After that we're going to close in prayer and head out the door going our separate ways.

I crossed the room to a classmate who had brightened my life with her laughter, and I told her so. I also said, "I hope you do take time to journal your experience with oral cancer. Your humor and indomitable spirit will bless many women."[8] Dr. Boseman taught me how to say goodbye, even though it's still my least favorite thing to do. Her words have guided me in releasing colaborers and dear friends as God calls them away through relocation or calls them "home" through death.

For Reflection

1. Seeking accountability is particularly important for leaders. What accountability do you already have in your life?

2. I once heard Howard Hendricks, a professor at Dallas Theological Seminary, pray that our church "may have faith and vision equal to our opportunities." How would you describe the meaning of that prayer?

3. Eugene Peterson said, "There's such intimacy in relationships of those you lead." What are some life experiences you've had the opportunity to share with sisters in Christ?

4. Jennifer Kennedy Dean describes the admonition to "pray without ceasing" as "living a praying life." It's being so filled with the Spirit of God that you live in a constant awareness of his presence. What is your understanding of the exhortation to "pray without ceasing?"

12

SUSTAINING FRESHNESS: FOR YOURSELF AND YOUR MINISTRY

Encouraged in heart and united in love.

Colossians 2:2

Macy, a single professional, looked for a place where she could both contribute and grow spiritually at her church. She investigated opportunities to get involved in women's ministry even though she didn't fit the assumed profile of married-with-kids. She added vitality to the leadership team with her writing and marketing background. She also brought awareness of her generation's life issues to the planning table along with creative ways to reach them. In addition, she served as a valuable link between women's ministry and single women of the church. Serving in leadership helped her to see beyond her singleness to the all-inclusive concept of women of the church.

Sustaining freshness and vitality in women's ministry requires continuing to do the basics, like prayer, Bible study, and outreach, but avoiding a "maintenance mindset." Bringing in perceptive women like Macy will help you see new ways to tackle old challenges. Perhaps just updating your image will create freshness. When we realized roses and tea cups didn't reflect the younger generation, we worked to identify a new look for our brochure. That year we went from red roses to whimsical caricatures of women in yellow, lime, and pink on the brochure! Maintaining freshness in ministry also includes avoiding a maintenance mentality.

Avoiding a Maintenance Mentality

Sometimes a specific ministry area loses vitality. When that happens, evaluate the areas that need attention. Does the time, location, or leadership need changing? Does the need for this ministry no longer exist? Leaders must be willing to temporarily or permanently set aside a floundering ministry and try something new if stagnation has set in. The leadership of our evening MOPS[1] group recently suggested they move their group from an evening to a morning. I was personally disappointed because our area has multiple day groups but no evening groups. I thought the working moms needed this enrichment opportunity just like the at-home moms. The leadership team had discovered the working moms enjoyed coming but didn't have time to commit to leadership. They also reminded me that every MOPS group in town had long waiting lists, and a new day group could meet that need. So we're now in the process of transitioning from an evening to a day group rather than fight the maintenance mentality of trying to keep an evening group going.

Margaret led a sewing ministry that met many unique needs within the community. One item, a smocked baby gown for stillborn premature babies born to mothers with AIDS, touched hearts in a special way. These tiny babies required clothing so small they had to use doll patterns. Gowns with matching bonnets and blankets allowed these grieving mothers to beautifully clothe their little ones in preparation for burial—layettes lovingly provided in the name of Jesus. Surprisingly, when Margaret, the sewing group's leader, moved, none of the members wanted to assume leadership. The group just decided to stop meeting until God provided a new leader. They literally locked the door to their supply closet, prayed, and waited. During the tenth month, a recently retired high school teacher with experience teaching sewing classes agreed to pray about this opportunity. Within weeks the sewing machines hummed once again. They had a fresh focus and began meeting an even wider variety of needs. Waiting on God's timing keeps freshness and vitality in his work!

Storming Brains

We've all heard that two heads are better than one, and it's true. Shirley Moses phoned me one day with an invitation to meet with women in leadership in the Dallas area for a "storming brains" session. "Storming brains" was a slip of the tongue but has now become the official title of her regular networking sessions! The energy of creativity provides a rich resource of mental electricity. I sat last year in a brainstorming session to develop an exciting concept. We all believed in it but didn't know how to go about bringing it into reality. We called it "Womenary."[2] We all knew we loved the whimsical word and we knew what we wanted to do—provide seminary type topics in a woman friendly format. We had six women talking all at once. What energy! What fun!

Writers for sitcoms literally sit around a table and play off one another's ideas until they come up with what they're looking for. I've decided creative planning times with leadership teams are my favorite strategy for maintaining vitality in women's ministry. We laugh at the absurd ideas but eventually end up with something new and fresh. During one of our last brainstorming sessions, we discovered younger women reacted either neutrally or negatively to the idea of a banquet. They suggested a woman's night out instead. After we tossed out lots of things to include for a night out, we decided women like three things: chocolate, shopping, and spending time with girlfriends. We settled on a chocolate buffet and a humorous speaker. We also invited some of our favorite shop owners to display some of their wares for a time of shopping. We planned it as a time for friends to gather and for those without a church home to hear the gospel in a seeker-sensitive environment. We called it Triple Treat—Girlfriends, Shopping, and Chocolate. We used a triple-decker ice cream cone for publicity. We sold all our tickets and had a waiting list, all because of a brainstorming session's valuable input from the younger generation.

Gathering with Leaders

Networking with other women in leadership builds relationships and strengthens each ministry. In many ways, it's just another form of brainstorming, only you'll find yourself asking questions like, "I'm running out of ideas for equipping my small group leaders. What do your leaders enjoy attending?" Networking ideas for speakers and events increases your own resource list. Perhaps you're discouraged as a leader and need a fresh vision from God. Visiting with another leader about personal issues lets you discover common struggles leaders face, like administrative, volunteer, and budget challenges.

Consider initiating networking if none exists in your area. If necessary, make a list of churches from your local yellow pages, then call and ask for a contact person for women's ministry. With a little effort, you'll soon have an effective network in place. Partnering with other churches' ministries in addressing specific needs like grief support groups, marriage enrichment, divorce recovery, and widowhood allows both ministries to expand their leadership base and address similar issues in both churches. This works especially well in smaller churches that might not have enough women to form a separate group. Even sharing decorations, table-

141

cloths, chairs, and tables saves money and time. In addition to maintaining freshness in ministry through networking and brainstorming, leaders must also maintain personal vitality.

Reading for Renewal

I have a two-foot stack of books in my bedroom that seems to call my name every time I pass by, saying, "Read me, read me!" It's such a personal source of frustration. Many of you can remember how few Christian books existed twenty years ago. Bible studies for women began arriving only ten years ago. I love to browse Christian bookstores and thumb through new releases. What a rich resource God has provided us! Fred Smith, executive director of Fourth Partner Foundation,[3] recently commented on one strategy for coping with the abundance of information and his time constraints: "I must now read for what I need to know rather than read for what I want to know." That helped me fine-tune the ongoing discriminating process. I now read for personal growth and for pleasure. I also want to know what the culture around me reads, but usually a good summary like *World* magazine[4] suffices.

Keeping Up with Technology

During the early years of our marriage, I remember asking my husband to replace a key on my college portable typewriter. He returned from the store announcing they no longer made replacement parts. He then proudly presented me with the forerunner of a personal computer. For months I struggled to master the technology and often just laid my head down on top of it and wept with frustration. I wondered why he didn't just get me a new typewriter. Today I enjoy the convenience of a laptop computer that allows me to connect wirelessly to the Internet, but I'll never forget the determined battle it took to cross that mental barrier and decide "I can and will do this!"

Reading *The Millennium Matrix* by M. Rex Miller has helped me understand the source of my frustration with technology. The author overviews how culture has historically impacted the church as it has moved from the oral culture (liturgical), the print culture (printed copies of the Bible), the broadcast culture (television), and now into the digital culture (computers). He calls this current shift a "turbulent, undefined zone of transition."[5] He adds, "We're not yet fully integrated into an interactive culture—perhaps some of us never will be."[6]

We read books and we watch television, but not all of us are comfortable with computers, personal digital assistants, and cell phones that also allow the user to send text messages and snapshots and surf the Web. Our self-consciousness about using these technologies negates their alluring power. Nevertheless, an entire generation will soon take these interactive technologies for granted. "They will look at television in the same way that baby boomers looked at radio—as outmoded and old-fashioned."[7]

These new digital technologies influence learning styles and all forms of communications. I recently received an email from a young woman I decided must have a language disability. I struggled through her emails for weeks before I finally realized she was using text-messaging lingo in her emails! Our singles' minister notes that younger singles prefer text messaging to leaving voice messages on his office phone. A summer intern keeps her entire calendar in her PalmPilot.

Even if you're comfortable with today's technology, being a lifelong learner means keeping up with new technology. Establishing a can-do attitude will keep you relevant as a leader. You'll be accessible to the younger generation and model for the others how to stay in touch with the culture. You won't have time to master everything you want to learn, but you'll start the process and be able to add skill upon skill.

We can refuse to move forward or we can go boldly into the future. It's our choice. Determine you can do it, take one step at a time, and seek out a *woman* who understands your frustrations to teach you.

Accessing Online Resources

Utilize online resources specifically designed to enhance ministries to women. Jennifer Rothschild and her husband publish an e-letter[8] to women in leadership. They pack it with ideas gathered from other women in leadership. Life-Way Christian Resources[9] also provides excellent online resources. Twelve women currently write for a women's daily devotional website, www.encouraging.com. The contributing authors enjoy hearing from women all over the world. Imagine, God can use one woman taking time to write down her thoughts about God and his Word to strengthen another woman on the other side of the planet—online. Mary Whelchel at ChristianWorkingWomen.org[10] emails a weekly devotional for working women. Many excellent websites[11] can guide you to additional resources. Additional sites[12] offer Bible study resources to assist you in your own study and teaching preparations. Rather than purchasing costly books, you can often accomplish your research online. Familiarize yourself with these resources, then introduce them to your leadership team. They're free and instantly available.

Avoiding Overload

Richard Swenson, M.D., author of *The Overload Syndrome*,[13] talks about personal limits and thresholds.

System overload is a reality. Everything in our world continues to escalate—including opportunities for ministry. Limitations of our humanity, though, remain unchanged. We need the same amount of sleep as the previous generations. We need nutritious food and pleasurable respite. We can try to squeeze in as much living as possible in our twenty-four-hour days, but when we cross the line of our human limitations, we experience genuine system overload.

I often reflect on the early days of ministry when I spoke at a large women's conference. I noticed the coordinator looked particularly harried. Her ensuing comment stunned me. "Each year in planning the conference I push so hard and do so much to make it better than the previous year that I always end up in the hospital afterwards. I just plan on that being my rest time in preparation for the next conference." God just couldn't be pleased with that strategy! Perhaps serving God makes us think we can supernaturally bypass those human limits, but we can't.

The Bible reminds us that we're housed in clay vessels. Paul writes in 2 Corinthians 4:6–7 that we have a treasure, "the light of the knowledge of the glory of God in the face of Christ," stored in "jars of clay." Why? "To show that this all-surpassing power is from God and not from us." God gets my attention when he points out our human limitations are the very limiting factor that demonstrates the power of God in our lives. We've heard the maxim, "When we can't, God can," but applying it to leadership just might be a new area of demonstrating faith. We must constantly check to see that we're filled with God's Holy Spirit and trusting him to accomplish his work—then waiting on his timing. Does trusting God mean we're lazy or don't want to do our part? No, it means acknowledging our human limits. We simply run out of hours and energy.

Suffering from overload means you're trusting in yourself rather than God. How many times have we weary Christians shook our heads in guilty recognition of Isaiah's penetrating question: "Do you not know? Have you not heard? The LORD is the everlasting God, the Creator of the ends of the earth. He will not grow tired or weary and his understanding no one can fathom" (Isa. 40:27–28). Isaiah writes of restoration to encourage the weary children of Israel. His words describing the everlasting God remain true for us today. "He gives strength to the weary and increases the power of the weak. Even youths grow tired and weary, and young men stumble and fall; but those who hope in the LORD will renew their strength. They will soar on wings like eagles; they will run and not grow weary, they will walk and not be faint" (vv. 29–31).

Taking Mood Breaks

When was the last time you pushed yourself to complete something, but you had a bad attitude the whole time? Perhaps you needed a mood break! One morning during Amber's weeklong stay with us, we saw the need for a mood break. Her eighteen-month-old daughter, Madison, came to breakfast and whined about everything. She didn't want to get in the highchair. She didn't want anything Amber offered her to eat. She didn't want to get dressed. I suggested that Amber take Madison back to the bedroom, close the door, turn off the lights, and just rock her. Madison needed a mood break, a fresh start on the day. Well, the second try at starting their day worked! Sometimes we also need to take a mood break. We need to walk away, do something else, take a nap, get a protein snack, or even exercise. We need time to allow God to reset our attitude.

I had to take a mood break just last week. Our church scheduled a home for demolition to make room for a parking lot. I asked permission for families from our mission church to retrieve fixtures, counters, cabinets, toilets, etc., beforehand. I envisioned all the happy homemakers getting replacement items for their homes. The morning of the day our harvesting was to occur, a bulldozer showed up and razed the building. I couldn't even find the emotional energy to drive past the pile of rubble. I despaired, and so did the families. Unfortunately, we must cope with miscommunication and human error as part of ministry. As I prayed through the incident and my mood, I felt the Lord watching me. He impressed upon me that my response to the incident was far more important than the incident itself. As I grieved for the women and their disappointment, I found solace in asking the Lord to meet their specific needs in another way. I acknowledged that his resources were unlimited. I found the peace I sought during my mood break.

Combating Busyness

Tim Kimmel spoke one summer during our week at family camp. He addressed busyness based on his book *Little House on the Freeway*.[14] I'll always remember my ten-year-old daughter saying, "Mom, he's talking about us. We really do live on a freeway!" She was right. Our house backed up to a four-lane highway. The horns and brakes of passing cars, trucks, and motorcycles constantly reminded us of the fast-paced world at our back door. We still live in that house, and I've learned to tune out the distractions of others, but I still struggle to combat my own tendency to pack my days too full. Sorting through demands of ministry requires prayerful discernment and a proactive determination to weed out unnecessary intrusions. Your leadership team can provide a healthy sounding board in the process. Managing busyness rather than allowing it to manage you will maintain vitality and freshness in your personal life and in ministry throughout the year.

Choose Prioritized Living

In *Women as Risk-Takers for God,*[15] Lorry Lutz says,

> It was quite a juggling act to be wife, mother of five children and missionary. While I knew pretty well what was expected of me as a wife and mother, the tension between responsibilities at home and the ministry was a constant frustration. Whose need was most urgent: the young blacks in Soweto who lived under the bondage of poverty, discrimination and spiritual darkness, or my own five with all the God-given potential waiting to be developed, and whom I loved so dearly?

Lorry concluded it must be possible to fulfill both responsibilities or God wouldn't have given both to her. Lorry consciously sought what I like to call a prioritized life.

A prioritized life differs from a balanced life. We don't divide up each day into equal portions between children, husband, home, and ministry. We arrange each day based on a wide variety of responsibilities and priorities based on timelines and God's leading. Instead of struggling to define a balanced life, seek to live a prioritized life—and set your priorities each morning as you spend time with the Giver of our days. Eugene Peterson translates King David's words in *The Message*:

> You have bedded me down in lush meadows,
>   you find me quiet pools to drink from.
> True to your word,
>   you let me catch my breath
>   and send me in the right direction.
>
> Psalm 23:2–3

Even a day planned with prayer still harbors the unexpected. I'm learning to respond to people interruptions without glancing at my watch or worrying about my to-do list. Oswald Chambers says in *My Utmost for His Highest*, "Never allow that the haphazard is anything less than God's appointed order."[16] It's taken the Lord many years to change my priorities from tasks and checklists to people needs as they present themselves. I'm beginning to trust the interruptions as "God's appointed order" for my day. Biddy Chambers, Oswald Chambers's wife, had her own ministry to women. After Oswald's death, she worked long, hard days running a boardinghouse as a young, single mother. Even during those demanding days, she consistently took time for any woman who needed her counsel and prayer. She called it her "ministry of the teapot." You too will begin to find the harmony and easy flow of a prioritized life as you trust each day to the God of peace.

For Reflection

1. Sustaining freshness and vitality in women's ministry requires continuing to do the basics, like prayer, Bible study, and outreach, yet avoiding a maintenance mindset at the same time. Describe how that is possible.

2. Leaders must be willing to temporarily or permanently set aside a floundering ministry area and to try something new if stagnation has set in. What, if any, areas of ministry in your church need reevaluating?

3. Networking informally by email or telephone plus meeting regularly with other women in leadership builds relationships and strengthens each ministry. Name women leaders that you have identified in your area.

4. Numerous online resources energize ministries to women. Describe one of your favorite online resources.

13

LEADING LEADERS

To the one who has been entrusted with much,
much more will be asked.

Luke 12:48

NANCY LODES

Nancy enjoys reflecting on how much she's grown in leadership skills since she yielded her life to Christ. She's focused on three general areas of equipping: teaching and speaking, lay counseling, and mentoring. She acquired some of her equipping outside her church, and other areas, like lay counseling, through her church's leadership training resources. God has used her skills both in group settings and in one-on-one settings. She's particularly passionate about mentoring in the areas of weight loss and abusive childhood issues. Nancy's faithfulness to personal equipping and sharing what she's learned with others continues to strengthen God's kingdom and bring glory to him.

Women in ministry must continue to grow personally as leaders and also invest in developing leadership skills in those they lead. They do that by sharing what they learn about leadership as they learn it. I consistently hear a common question, "How does a woman in leadership know how to do what she does?" I've asked that question of many leaders myself, and they all seem to say something similar: "Most days I wake up feeling inadequate for the responsibilities I face. During my time with the Lord in his Word and in prayer, I always feel encouraged by God's adequacy. He reminds me that I don't need to be adequate. In fact, it's my inadequacy that drives me to dependency on God."

I pass those same words of encouragement on to you. It's your inadequacy that causes you to find your adequacy in Christ. Let those feelings drive you to him. Ask him to provide the wisdom you need. My informal strategy for leading is to make sure the Holy Spirit is in control of all areas of my life, and then be willing to feel like I'm flying by the seat of my pants! Godly leaders simply make themselves available as God's hand, heart, and mouth in any particular situation. Paul said it this way: "[The Lord] said to me, 'My grace is sufficient for you, for my power is made perfect in weakness.' . . . For when I am weak, then I am strong" (2 Cor. 12:9–10).

Learning from Respected Leaders

Whom do you admire in leadership? Who has a particular skill you'd like to acquire? It's a common practice in the business world to learn from others who have skills you seek. Seek out other leaders who can serve as personal mentors. People have debated for decades the question, "Are leaders born or made?" I've seen supporting evidence for both positions. It's actually a useless discussion in the kingdom of God. God not only calls, but he also equips. If he's called you to lead, he'll furnish you with what you need. We marvel at the strength Esther[1] demonstrated as queen during the reign of Xerxes. God used a beauty contest to place her in one of the most influential positions of her day. Her influence literally saved the Jews from eradication. She learned much from her God, from her uncle Mordecai, and from Hegai, the eunuch in charge of the harem. What do you want to learn, and who do you know who possesses that character quality or leadership skill?

I've sought mentoring from many people through the years: Debbie Stewart taught me the importance of networking. Vicki Neil coached me in working alongside men. Bobbie Burks instructed me on boundary setting, and Marge Lenow influenced budgeting skills. Ken Warren taught me goal setting, and Carye Gillen showed me how to organize a conference. I caught Jaye Martin's passion for women and evangelism and Margaret Kennedy's delight in studying and applying God's Word. The list is endless, and the point is clear: leaders are learners who learn from others.

Even casual conversations can provide mentoring opportunities. I sat in a circle of women in leadership when the facilitator asked one of the participants to close in prayer. As she prayed, she never closed her eyes or bowed her head. I'll always remember her response when I asked why she prayed with her eyes open. She replied, "I had my eyes open? Hmmm. I wasn't aware of that. We have many new believers in our church who have come out of abusive relationships. They feel vulnerable when they close their eyes to pray. We've learned to encourage them to pray in whatever way they feel most comfortable. We have so many women with these issues that often we all just keep our eyes open. It's become so natural, I wasn't even aware that I had them open just now." That brief conversation as a young leader with a seasoned leader showed me sensitivity and grace in leadership. I remember breathing a prayer to one day have that same depth of God's grace expressed through me.

I attended a similar leadership conference along with Pamela Reeves[2] when a blizzard knocked out electricity and turned the grounds into an icy wonderland. We all bundled up to walk down snowy sidewalks and up icy steps to breakfast. As Pamela and I walked together, I asked her why someone of her advanced years would brave the weather and hardships of travel to attend this conference. She answered, "You never get too old to learn. I just keep going forward in faith." I marveled and asked the Lord for a similar plucky attitude when and if I reached that same season of life.

Investing in a Leadership Team

One of the best ways to lead leaders is through your leadership team. George Barna, a Christian statistician, writes about team building and offers some helpful guidelines. He believes you build a strong leadership team through diversity. Leaders typically select others just like themselves. There's just a natural affinity among the like-minded. But a diversity of perspectives and personalities provides a stronger foundation. So resist the urge to recruit those just like you.

He also addressed a common concern among leaders—getting women to commit to leadership responsibilities. As a result, they worry their team is too small. George Barna actually suggests four members as the ideal size for a leadership team. The larger it grows after that means more difficulty coming to agreements and a longer time required for meetings. He considers a team of four streamlined and efficient. If your leadership team feels unruly and cumbersome, allow some of the members to rotate off and bring the count down to a more manageable size. If God has only provided you with three or four members, relax and enjoy efficiency!

Giving Team Members a Voice

By studying the diversity of the women in your church, you'll discover which groups to represent on your team. Typically you'll find stay-at-home moms, working women, and retirees as the largest groups. Jill Briscoe refers to these diverse subgrouping of women as "tribes." She says,

> Thirty years ago, when I first started to reach out to women through a women's ministry program, there was simply one group of women. I started a Bible study with six women and it eventually grew to eight hundred. I stood up, taught the Scriptures, and then went home. But things have changed. You have to do your homework. Women are more like tribes

155

now. There's a tribe of young mothers, there's a tribe of widows, there's a tribe of women who work outside the home, and there's a tribe of divorced women. Each tribe has its own culture, language, dress, thought process, and needs. What attracts a young mother will not necessarily attract a widow or a divorced woman. To reach women, we often have to understand their contemporary culture.[3]

I love Jill's quote. It communicates the ever-increasing complexity of our culture. When you consider reaching women, you'll also need to consider their "tribe." The stay-at-home moms even subdivide into moms who homeschool, moms with kids attending private schools, and moms with kids in public schools. The working women also subdivide. They represent CEOs and superintendents as well as hourly workers and women with home businesses. You'll also discover differing needs among the single women—single and never married, divorced with children, divorced with no children, and widowed. The widowed women further subdivide. Widows are young and still working or retired and alone at home. As a leader building a team, ask God to point you to those largest groups of women and someone within those groups who is willing to provide a voice for their needs. With time, you'll see an amazing thing happen. God will begin calling out women in one tribe or season of life to reach out to those in another. It'll be the body of Christ in action. But for now, begin your focus with the largest three or four groups.

Training Opportunities for Leaders

Stay alert for opportunities to offer leadership training for those you lead. Currently, LifeWay Christian Publishers[4] and Group Publishing[5] equip women to lead through seminars and conferences scheduled throughout the United States and Canada. Many of the larger churches like Willow Creek[6] and Elmbrook[7] also provide opportunities for leadership development. The market continues to produce excellent resources through books and DVDs. Ask your team what specific topics they'd like to study, like decision making, problem solving, or conflict resolution, then look for resources. They might be right there in your own church or community. New skills renew and invigorate your team. This also lets them know how seriously you take their commitment to leadership. As you begin to develop your budget, remember to add leadership training as an annual expense. It's an investment with big returns.

Consider bringing in a consultant rather than taking your leadership team to a conference. This offers an economical option that also meets the need of busy women. Look for someone who might spend an evening or morning answering questions and sharing new ideas with your team. Even a leadership lunch can contribute new ways of approaching an old problem. One year we brought in Marge Lenow, women's ministries director from Bellevue Baptist Church in Memphis, to spend a Friday evening and Saturday morning with our team. We gathered in a lakeside home for a loosely structured agenda that allowed us the freedom to discuss new ideas as they came up. Marge helped us plan for the future by helping us think through our next level of organizational needs.

Identifying Skewed Priorities

I once read that up to 80 percent of people employed in caregiving professions, like nursing, social work, or religious work, come from dysfunctional backgrounds. I immediately wanted to know why. I've learned that the positive feedback received from someone they've helped "feels good." It's affirming and gives a quick fix to a sagging sense of personal value. The recovery community uses the word *caretaking* in place of the word *caregiving* to describe this behavior. Positive feedback actually motivates the care and attention given to others. Leaders influenced by these unhealthy motives lack the discernment required to set priorities. Their own need to rescue and take care of other women prevents them from knowing how to sort through conflicting demands. As a leader, you can help those you lead to discern their own personal motives and seek the personal growth they need to minister out of a full heart rather than an empty tank.

Discerning daily priorities also requires knowing how to set healthy boundaries. I first realized my own limitations in understanding boundaries after I picked up the book *Boundaries*[8] by Henry Cloud and John Townsend. I panicked after reading the first chapter, "A Day in a Life without Boundaries." The anxiety set in when I realized I didn't see anything abnormal about the day. I immediately skipped to the back of the book and read the last chapter, "A Day in a Life with Boundaries." What a difference healthy boundaries made! If you suspect weak boundaries as part of your leadership frustration, begin the process of understanding and putting them into place. You'll increase your effectiveness as a leader as you learn to prioritize each day's responsibilities and as you set healthy limits in responding to others' expectations.

Leadership in the Marketplace

Working full-time outside of the home doesn't mean you can't assume women's leadership responsibilities. It's challenging but not impossible. I listened intently to Sheila talk about her adventures in real estate and in women's ministry leadership. She personally invests in her leadership team and encourages them as they fulfill their individual responsibilities. She's learned to be focused and intentional with her time and equipping. She also believes that equipping women in the workplace to see their environment as a personal mission field is a major portion of leadership development.

Statistics vary from church to church, but the average church has around 60 percent of their female membership in the workplace. I know one church with 100 percent! In contrast, churches located in retirement communities may have a very low percentage. Regardless of your church's personal profile, look for ways to invest in these women as leaders. As you investigate opportunities to challenge and equip them, it'll strengthen their commitment to be salt and light to those around them. Stephen Graves and Thomas Addington communicate a basic principle in their book, *The Fourth Frontier.*[9] Helping women feel God's call upon each of their days in the workplace will assist them in integrating their work with their witness. They'll begin to feel a personal accountability to influence their workplace for Christ.

If you struggle with finding common ground for leadership opportunities for both homemakers and working women, allow them to develop separate and distinct identities. Allow them to be individual tribes. Their needs vary greatly between each group. Each places high value on their free time and typically respond to options they feel meet specific personal needs.

Locating Mentors in Books

I'm always amazed at the books God uses to speak to a particular need in my life. What a blessing to live in an era of abundant printed resources. I've found many mentors in books, and you will too. I encourage you to begin building a personal library of books on leadership. Don't let finances limit you. Borrow books or purchase used copies off the Internet. Don't overlook yard sales. I love to stop at ones in my neighborhood. I always look first for the book box and usually leave with several new treasures. It's a wonderful way to discover the heart of many great leaders you'll never have a chance to meet in person. Encourage your own leadership team to read. I recently discovered a seminary only thirty miles away that opens their library to the public. I'm considering scheduling a day trip with interested members of our leadership team. We'll spend a morning browsing the bookshelves and lunchtime sharing what we've learned. We'll also nurture responsible stewardship of the resources God's provided us. And of course, any library that participates in interlibrary loan can get you just about anything you want, and you never have to travel far from home.

For Reflection

1. Women in ministry must continue to grow personally as leaders and also to invest in developing leadership skills in those they lead. What leadership skill would you like to work on this next year?

2. Whom do you admire in leadership? What particular leadership skills do you admire in them?

3. One of the best ways to lead leaders is through your leadership team. Name some women you'd like to have on your leadership team. Pause and ask God to begin speaking to their hearts about this need.

4. Discerning daily priorities also requires knowing how to set healthy boundaries. What is your understanding of a personal boundary?

14

Developing Generational Leaders

Do not forsake me, O God,
till I declare your power to the next generation,
your might to all who are to come.

Psalm 71:17–18

Carrie discovered the joy of knowing Christ as her Savior as a young adult in college. Within a short time, she realized God wanted to touch the pain of her past with his healing love. Eventually the Lord burdened her with the need to reach her own generation with the challenge of seeking sexual purity and godliness. She visited with her women's minister about ways God might use her to invite others to join her on this quest. Together they faced an uncharted course as they investigated new ways to impact lives of young adult women with God's call to holiness.

D eveloping leaders within each generation of women requires understanding the long-term benefits of generational leadership. It also requires intentional focus. I'm intrigued by the distinctions between how my children and how my husband and I view the world around us. The words we each use to communicate offer clear examples of our different perspectives. My youngest daughter recently reacted with, "Mother! I can't believe you said that!" I'd mentioned the struggles of a young woman who'd had a child out of wedlock. I offended Lisa with the phrase "out of wedlock." Lisa corrected me with, "Say 'a single mother'!

Nobody uses the phrase 'out of wedlock' anymore!" I've since pointed out the more sensitive phrasing numerous times to my peers. We want to build bridges to the generations coming behind us. We want to see God produce leaders in each age group of women. It's appropriate to remind ourselves, "It's not about us!" The body of Christ functions as a whole, incorporating the gifts and contributions of all generations. We want the body of Christ to operate effectively on all levels. Ken Hemphill describes the breadth of the body of Christ this way: "The kingdom in community is the visible picture of God's grace in the world. Through the collective witness of our shared faith, we do more to showcase God's glory than all of our personal acts and accolades could achieve in a lifetime."[1]

Avoiding Generational Tunnel Vision

Each of us sees the world through our limited perspective. Peer culture, life experiences, educational and economic level, world events, gender, and temperament all affect our viewpoint. It's only natural to think our perspective is the only right perspective. It's what we know! We must daily resist this egocentric temptation. Only a Spirit-filled mind has the selfless ability to see life from someone else's perspective. Freeing your mind and biases to view life from each generation's perspective allows you to extend grace and to empower leaders in each age group in the church.

Just look around and notice what you see to discover the varying generational perspectives represented in your church. Look forward and then look backward in increments of ten years. Examples are as close as your immediate family. My parents represented a generation who grew up in the waning years of the Depression and bore the hardships of World War II. Both of my parents found strength and hope in their neighborhood church. The hymns they sang each

Sunday offered solace and familiarity in an unpredictable time. It's easy to see what they valued and needed from their spiritual community. Women within that age group led quietly behind the scenes and relied heavily on prayer.

Mary Lynn Thompson just retired from forty years of teaching in Bible Study Fellowship[2] and continues to teach in Sunday morning Bible study. She was just the woman I needed to encourage and bless our small group leadership. I asked her to share her calling to work with women and why she invested forty years of her life doing just that. I wanted her to encourage our leaders in their high calling and pray a prayer of blessing on their individual small group ministries. What a joy to see the radiant testimony of a life well lived. We must access this generation of leaders while we can. We can also minister to them by encouraging and assisting them as they face the increasing challenges of health and independent living.

Do you have a close friend or family member in their early retirement years? Think of their world and how they would most effectively reach their peers with the relevancy of Christ's love and kingdom needs. How can they be creatively challenged to use their newfound freedoms for Christ? What are empty nesters facing? What vulnerabilities and availabilities do those women confront? If you don't know, ask one. Who but another empty nester could best challenge them to consider God's call upon their lives? Examine the world of women who keep up with the demands of teenagers, a career, and the encroaching needs of an aging mother or mother-in-law. Who could best speak to their needs? Women who feel the overwhelming challenge and exhaustion of parenting young children need to see a peer committed to seeking God in the midst of these challenges. They need to know someone really and truly understands the unique mommy-pressures of their generation. What about the single women who think all happiness lies in marriage and kids? Who can best communicate to the young professionals seeking fulfillment in climbing the corporate ladder? Can you speak their language? Do you know their vocabulary? You can build bridges, pray for them, and love them, but you serve them best by challenging them to lead out in their peer group as women seeking God's heart.

Identifying Leaders

As we look for leaders within each generation, we sometimes get confused by the world's definition of a leader—a sharp, take-charge, well-respected person. We clarify our mission by looking at how Jesus led and at what the Bible says about those he calls. Jesus had a gentle spirit, but he also had a straightforward approach to speaking truth. He spent long days ministering to others but then spent time alone to renew his strength. He communicated a key leadership quality when he washed the disciples' feet and said, "Now that I, your Lord and Teacher, have washed your feet, you also should wash one another's feet. I have set you an example that you should do as I have done for you" (John 13:14–15).

Earlier, the disciples had become indignant with James and John who wanted positions of honor in Christ's coming kingdom. Jesus called them together for a time of clarification about what it meant to be a true follower of Christ. He drew clear distinctions between the ways of man and the ways of God.

> You know that the rulers of the Gentiles lord it over them, and their high officials exercise authority over them. Not so with you. Instead, whoever wants to become great among you must be your servant, and whoever wants to be first must be your slave—just as the Son of Man did not come to be served, but to serve, and to give his life as a ransom for many.
>
> Matthew 20:25–28

165

As you look for women leaders, look first for a servant's heart. Visit with them personally and share with them the leadership qualities you see in them. Find out what's on their hearts or what unaddressed needs they're seeing among their friends. Challenge them to pray and think about opportunities within women's ministry to influence others and make a difference in the kingdom of God.

Extending a Personal Challenge

I'll always remember receiving a phone call from our women's minister with a desperate request: the women's retreat speaker had canceled—would I take her place? Even more surprising, she gave me an assigned topic. I was a young mom with four kids under ten years and with very little experience or time to prepare. "I don't know anything about spiritual gifts." I couldn't believe her response: "Well, you have three months to learn all you can!" That was 1985, and I still marvel that she had the courage to entrust such a huge responsibility to someone so young and inexperienced. That's exactly how leaders develop. You entrust them with responsibilities. I worked tirelessly in preparation because someone trusted me to do a good job.

It's so easy to ask the same people over and over because they have a track record. When was the last time you challenged someone other than a friend or someone who always says yes? When we call upon the same women, we face the possibility of creating burnout. We also face the liability of failing to develop new leadership. No matter the size of your church, you'll constantly confront the challenge of getting to know new women. My pastor likes to say, "No matter the size of the church, you'll typically be able to maintain relationships with only about forty to fifty people." If this is true, then accept the challenge of constantly meeting and developing relationships with potential leaders outside your immediate circle of relationships. Resist the comfort of recruiting the familiar and faithful few.

Learn to go to your leadership team for assistance in meeting leadership needs. Ask small group leaders to suggest women they've gotten to know through their studies. When someone provides me with the name of a potential leader, I give that person a call, tell her who gave me her name, and invite her to visit with me about a specific area of responsibility. Even if the time is not right for her to commit, I've gotten to know her and have fine-tuned my understanding of where her interests lie. I also keep a record of these contacts. I keep an index box where I write down any and everything I might want to retrieve at a future date. It's such a simple system I hesitate even mentioning it to you. It would be more impressive to say I have all this information stored in my PalmPilot. The truth is, this system works well for me. I also keep a notepad in my purse. Anytime a woman mentions she's interested in a specific area of service, I write it down immediately. I later stick it in my box. Months later, I may have forgotten the woman's name, but I can always retrieve it by thumbing through the cards. Look for a system that works for you, because each contact, no matter how brief, has the potential for developing new leadership.

Empowering

Entrusting and empowering means you as the leader must be willing to set aside personal control issues and the need to receive the credit. You must also be willing to accept responsibility for all the random mishaps that typically occur with new leadership. That's one of the reasons it's difficult to resist the temptation to call on the same women each time. They work well together. They know their tasks as well as the procedures. Every leader dreams of having a smoothly running team that requires no coaching, but it won't develop leadership abilities in the next generation.

I'll always remember one particular opening day of our Tuesday morning Bible study. We had a new helper responsible for making the coffee. She placed a single sign by each of the coffeepots. Rather than writing "decaf" or "regular," she wrote "guess." When I asked her what "guess" meant, she said she couldn't remember which was which, so she just put a "guess" sign on both! Fortunately, she eventually worked out a personal system for making coffee, but expect new leadership to usually have their "uh-oh" moments. Learn to take deep breaths and enjoy them. You can also ease transitions in leadership by bringing in women as apprentices. Regardless of what strategy you use, you eventually still have to let go. God has been doing just that generation after generation for over two thousand years. He trusted us with kingdom responsibilities when we had no track record, and we can learn to trust others in the same way.

Adding Summer Internships

Summer internship positions expose college students to the dynamics of leadership within a church setting. What an incredible opportunity! If your church doesn't already have an internship program, ask about starting one. Many college students continue to take summer classes but would also enjoy working part-time in your ministry area. Begin wherever God opens the door. Maybe they'll need to serve in a volunteer basis at first, but what a great work experience for a young person to add to their résumé. In addition, some high school students need volunteer hours for their honors classes. You'll also be able to serve as a personal reference when they graduate and apply for their first full-time job.

Perhaps they could job-share, working with the student ministry ten hours and women's ministry ten hours. Begin negotiating and trust that God will begin that generational ministry training in his timing.

Our first intern wasn't a college youth but a high school teacher. She worked on a seminary degree during the summer months, preparing to serve in ministry when she retired. One class required supervised work in a local church. What a treat to have her as a resource that summer. She needed a project for her class, and I had an idea just waiting for someone with time and energy to implement   a resource for women recently diagnosed with breast cancer. Another church in town had begun this ministry for their membership years earlier, and our women had requested something similar. Debbie compiled personal testimonies from breast cancer survivors from our church membership along with a reading list and sheets of helpful hints for family members. *The Tender Touch Gift Folder* has served as a valuable resource for women beginning their breast cancer journey. The folder has also provided friends a sensitive way to reach out in love to another woman.

Considering Girls' Ministry

Until several years ago, women's ministry focused solely on the needs of women in the local church. Today God is prompting women to look for strategic ways to reach out to girls as well. Sometimes they organize this ministry under student ministry, women's ministry, or a combination of both. One resource states:

Girls' ministry is a proactive way to instill godly values in young women while addressing the needs and issues they face. It can also be a preventative type of ministry. When girls establish their identities and values on God's Word as teens, they are well on their way to becoming godly women and avoiding the pitfalls (and consequences) so many of their peers may fall into as adults.[3]

Women can also support or sponsor a conference for girls like SAGE,[4] or Vicki Courtney's Yada Yada events.[5] Lisa Bevere, author of *Kissed the Girls and Made Them Cry,*[6] also has a passionate message for girls about purity. Pay attention to how God is working in this area and be sensitive to opportunities to join with him in encouraging godliness in this impressionable generation.

Embrace Budding Leadership

Most churches organize activities under the supervision of a staff member, even if that person provides only minimal supervision. I recently discovered a group of young moms meeting on our church campus Thursday evenings for a ten-week Bible study on parenting. I wondered why I didn't know about it. I typically would have helped them reserve a room and order workbooks. They'd accomplished those things on their own and were having a great time. Wonderful! Here were young moms desiring to raise godly children, and they'd taken the initiative to schedule a study that met their specific needs. Rejoice when you see that happening, and then invite them to call on women's ministry for future needs. I offered to help with future scheduling, ordering books, and even sharing additional resources. I wanted to invest in their natural initiatives and embrace the spontaneity of new leadership rather than reprimanding or enforcing church protocol. I also knew this age group is quick to circumvent rules and regulations if necessary to accomplish their goals.

Embracing these young moms builds bridges and facilitates what God is doing in the twenty-first-century church.

George Barna profiled this emerging generation of Christians in his book *Revolution*. He describes them as

> a demographically diverse group of people who are determined to let nothing stand in the way of an authentic and genuine experience with God. They are involved in a variety of activities and connections designed to satisfy a spiritual focus. They are God-lovers and joyfully obedient servants. They are willing to do whatever it takes to draw closer to God, to bond with Him, and to bring Him glory and pleasure. If that can be accomplished through existing structures and processes, they accept that; if not, they will blaze new trails to facilitate such a Spirit-driven life.[7]

This emerging generation of Christians will seek out and find what they want rather than passively sit by and accept what's offered. That's good news! Let's be sensitive to hear their requests and respond as quickly and effectively as possible.

Looking for ways to develop leadership in all generations challenges us to see with new eyes as we look for creative opportunities to challenge them. It's this very leadership, though, that will guide women in ministering to needs within the body of believers and also outside of the church walls in the community, the nation, and the world.

For Reflection

1. Only a Spirit-filled mind has the selfless ability to see life from someone else's perspective. What is your understanding of the difference between sympathy and empathy?

2. As we look for leaders within each generation, we can clarify our mission by looking at how Jesus led. Describe Jesus's style of leadership.

171

3. Entrusting and empowering means you as the leader must be willing to set aside personal control issues and the need to receive the credit. What experiences have you had with delegating responsibilities?

4. Leaders must also be willing to accept responsibility for all the random mishaps that typically occur with new leadership. Describe a new leader's recent mishap that you had to resolve.

PART IV

PROCLAIMING HIS MESSAGE

God calls leaders to reproduce themselves in those they lead. That includes looking for ways to share with others God's amazing plan for our salvation. As you send out and support other women, you grow in your awareness of God working in all parts of the world. Your devotion to serving our amazing God will begin to reproduce itself in the lives of women you lead. They too will want to join you in serving and proclaiming the message of Jesus Christ with their love, time, and energy.

15

REACHING OUTWARD through MEETING NEEDS

Let us consider how we may spur one another
on to love and good deeds.

Hebrews 10:24

Shelli found strength as the mother of a special needs daughter by connecting with other mothers facing the same challenges. Before long, she began writing newsletters and organizing informal gatherings. The group of moms soon outgrew their ability to meet in homes, so Shelli asked permission for the group to move under the umbrella of the women's ministry of her local church. They soon moved their monthly meetings to Tuesday mornings, the same day as other Bible studies. That allowed them to have access to childcare. Shelli's need to connect with other women naturally progressed into a unique ministry that benefited from the support of her church's women's ministry.

Matthew addresses the importance of meeting needs in a poignant passage late in his Gospel (25:37–40). Jesus says the righteous ones will ask him, "Lord, when did we see you hungry and feed you, or thirsty and give you something to drink? When did we see you a stranger and invite you in or needing clothes and clothe you? When did we see you sick or in prison and go to visit you?" Jesus answers their questions with jarring simplicity: "I tell you the truth, whatever you did for one of the least of these brothers of mine, you did for me." Sometimes these expressions of God's love within the body of Christ happen spontaneously, but other times they require planning.

Moving beyond Church Walls

As women receive nurturing, discipling, and equipping, they'll naturally begin to seek opportunities to reach outward to the community and beyond. Jesus exhorts us to shine in a dark world. Matthew records Jesus's familiar words in chapter 5:

> You are the light of the world. A city on a hill cannot be hidden. Neither do people light a lamp and put it under a bowl. Instead they put it on its stand, and it gives light to everyone in the house. In the same way, let your light shine before men, that they may see your good deeds and praise your Father in heaven.
>
> verses 14–16

I like the additional clarity of *The Message* translation:

> You're here to be light, bringing out the God-colors in the world. God is not a secret to be kept. We're going public with this, as public as a city on a hill. If I make you light-bearers, you don't think I'm going to hide you under a bucket, do you? I'm putting you on a light stand. Now that I've put you there on a hilltop, on a light stand—shine! Keep open house; be generous with your lives. By opening up to others, you'll prompt people to open up with God, this generous Father in heaven.

Few articles have had such a sobering effect as one I recently read entitled "Where to Now? Women as a Mission Field." Diane Langberg writes:

Do you know that females make up approximately one-half of the world's population? That means if we take the terrible plagues, such as abuse and trafficking, seriously, females comprise the largest mission field in this world. What might happen if the Church caught the vision of that field and began training and sending men and women around the world to protect, educate, nurture and rescue women and girls in the Name of Jesus?[1]

It's easier to explain away why we can't go long distances to minister, but Langberg also includes sobering statistics about women in the United States, women living right up the street from us:

Most studies suggest that one in three or one in four females experiences sexual abuse by the age of eighteen. Rape, one of the most underreported of all crimes, is believed to happen to one in four women. . . . Nearly 25% of women have been raped and/or physically assaulted by an intimate partner. About 80% of women in the workforce will experience sexual harassment at some point. In the wealthiest and most powerful country in the world, being born female is still something of a risk.[2]

Our commissioning is clear, and opportunities abound, but working out the logistics requires intentional prayer, planning, solid information about needs, and searching out opportunities to make a difference in the name of Jesus Christ.

Reaching Out in Small Churches

Regardless of the size of the church, gifted women reach out to those around them as God leads. If you feel your church is not large enough to make a significant impact in your community, resist that thought. It's not from God. You have lots of options. I just read in today's local newspaper

178

about a mission community outreach project lasting one week.[3] Three churches joined together to accomplish projects. They repaired five houses, built one new house, hosted a neighborhood festival, plus completed what they called "Tiny Tasks" repair projects. This is the twentieth year of the partnership. They also include daily work projects called "Just for Kids" workshops. Joint efforts are productive and fun. Find out how other churches are meeting community needs and join them. You can also provide opportunities for women in your church to start their own ministry. Church-run clothes closets and coats-for-kids drives offer examples of opportunities to shine your light.

I received a phone call one day from a family practitioner who had a special needs young adult client. The physician wanted her client to begin structuring her weekdays and asked if women's ministry could provide a weekly volunteer activity. Our special volunteer has now brightened our Thursday mornings for over four years. She's a delightful young woman in her early thirties. Her autism limits her ability to function comfortably in unpredictable surroundings, but her humor and cheerful attitude enrich our Thursday mornings. Scheduling her morning visit requires very little outside preparations but makes a big difference in her life.

Meeting Needs of the Displaced

Daily news makes us aware of the hardships of refugees due to wars, famines, earthquakes, and floods. Yet displacement issues exist in nearly every community. Almost weekly I address the housing needs of women facing divorce, leaving an abusive marriage, or integrating back into society after incarceration.

The world watched in 2005 as the levees broke in New Orleans during hurricane Katrina. We watched the dramatic

179

rescues from rooftops by helicopter and boats. I was stirred out of my hypnotic state when evacuees began arriving by bus at our church doorstep! The logistics of providing bedding, meals, and clean clothing for 150 individuals initially overwhelmed us. After those on the front lines met basic needs, the women's ministry looked at ways to provide "soul care" for the women refugees. We decided to offer one-on-one prayer each morning from ten to eleven. Eight women volunteered to attend an orientation preparing them for the types of stories they might hear. The orientation also reinforced guidelines for knowing when to contact professionals for stress intervention. We set up a prayer and hospitality room and extended personal invitations to the women. I'll always remember one precious elderly lady carefully ironing a pair of stained cotton slacks before she came for prayer. She worked as if ironing the queen's royal gown. As she moved the iron back and forth, she said, "Yes, I surely do want to go pray with you. The Lord has been so good to me. I'm not worried about all I lost. If the Lord provided once, he'll surely provide again. There's no need to worry. No need to worry at all." As we prayed with the women, the stories both blessed and broke our hearts. We saw God's comfort and provision at work as we joined with the body of Christ in assisting with food, shelter, clean clothes, job searches, and compassionate prayer.

Offering a Hand Up, Not a Hand Out

Many years ago I heard about a Christian-based pilot program designed to assist women in moving from financial dependency into the workforce. Such a huge undertaking intrigued me. Every time I read an article, I'd save it. I eventually heard about training offered in a neighboring city for women supervising this type of outreach. Our leadership team decided to send someone to investigate. At the last minute our attendee had a conflict and canceled. I wandered distraught into Sandra Mitcham's office, the missions administrative assistant. I casually asked if she'd like to attend the training. As I discussed the ministry profile, I noticed tears running down her cheeks. "Of course I'll go," she said. "God called me to this type of ministry ten years ago, and I haven't been able to figure out how to do it!" Sandra began a Christian Women's Job Corp[4] program that following year and has influenced many women's lives over the past eight years. I've encouraged Sandra, recruited volunteers, attended graduation ceremonies, and prayed through the ongoing challenges as Sandra led the ministry. God gives women in leadership influential opportunities to assist the body of Christ in accomplishing God's work on earth. I never tire of the challenge, and you won't either.

Offer support and encouragement as women see needs around them and want to reach out in response. Remind them and yourself to trust God's timing. If your heart is in tune with God's heart and if you're faithfully going to him in prayer, God will raise up the leadership and resources when he's ready to act. God develops within leaders the ability to dream God's dreams and an opportunity to play a key role in seeing those dreams accomplished—though not necessarily "your" way. You're the encourager and facilitator of seeing others accept responsibilities of leadership. I'm currently praying that God will identify someone to provide leadership for a Magdalene Ministry[5] in our community. The Magdalene Project reaches out to exotic dancers and prostitutes through the simple strategy of gift bags. I desire to see a children's clothes exchange among our young mothers. I also dream of a modified version of TV's *Extreme Makeover* that blesses a single mother through cosmetic updates and light repairs for her home. What are some of your dreams? Even if you don't have the energy or time to lead them yourself, you can pray for God to identify someone with administrative gifts and the desire to let her light shine.

181

For Reflection

1. As women receive nurturing, discipling, and equipping, they'll naturally begin to seek opportunities to reach outward to the community and beyond. In what ways are the women already doing that? What additional opportunities are you aware of?

2. Regardless of the size of the church, women can reach out to those around them. When was the last time you participated in a joint outreach effort?

3. Based on current statistics, the issues of abuse and trafficking mean females comprise the largest mission field in this world. What do you see happening if the church caught the vision of that field of ministry opportunities?

4. God gives women in leadership influential opportunities to assist the body of Christ in accomplishing God's work on earth. Reflect on a recent opportunity you had to influence ministry opportunities.

16

SHARING YOUR FAITH

You shine like stars in the universe
as you hold out the word of life.

Philippians 2:15

Laschel, a young mother with a heart for evangelism, challenged the moms in her Bible study group to share the good news of Christ with Hispanic moms at the city park. They arrived at the park at a previously arranged time and location. After gathering in groups of two, one woman initiated conversation with a Hispanic woman by offering homemade cookies packaged with an evangelistic tract. Her partner entertained the children by making a simple balloon animal. Afterward, the moms regathered and visited while the kids played. Laschel also led this same group of moms to designate one week a month of their Bible study time to sort clothes at their church's clothes closet.

God commissioned the church to share the message of God's salvation when he said, "Go into all the world and preach the good news to all creation" (Mark 16:15). Every believer has a responsibility to pass on the message someone faithfully shared with them. We're recipients of the same gospel the earliest followers of Christ shared over two thousand years ago. We must assume responsibility for keeping this process in motion. Fortunately, or unfortunately, the women you lead will generally reflect your personal attitude toward evangelism. If you don't already have a desire to seek out these types of opportunities for the women you lead, ask God to develop this response in your heart. He's always the source of everything we need. Consider yourself a learner just like those you lead. In addition, look for women who've participated in evangelism and outreach and ask them to provide leadership in this area.

Evangelistic Praying

Equipping women for sharing their faith begins with evangelistic prayer. Prayer prepares the way for God to act in drawing others to himself. Women are often more willing to pray than they are willing to share their personal stories. Learning to pray evangelistically is a good way to ease hesitant women into reaching friends and family for Christ. One resource for women called *Heartcall*[1] offers a four-week study designed for women to pray for family and friends who don't know the saving grace of Christ. It also equips them to share Christ when they have an opportunity.

Consider challenging the women to participate in the National Day of Prayer[2] each May. Investigate your denominational resources for praying for workers, nations, and ethnic groups around the world. Many organizations working alongside the local church, like Campus Crusade for Christ,[3] offer numerous prayer resources. Host prayer teas[4] for Muslim women or consider focusing on needs of any other religious group God lays on your heart. Encourage women to keep prayer journals to serve as prayer reminders as well as a place to document answered prayers.

Sharing Your Story

I'll never forget the moment when a high school classmate asked me how to become a Christian. My response still embarrasses me. I said, "I'm sure you can. I'll ask my pastor about that." I remember the feelings of inadequacy and the searching look in my friend's eyes. I determined right then that would never happen again. Through the years, I've learned how God uses each person's personal experience of accepting his free gift of salvation as an avenue for sharing Christ's saving love with others. Our stories make the gospel personal, and women listen attentively and respecfully.

Dan Allender believes in the power of our personal life story. He writes:

> God is not simply the Creator of our lives. He is also the Author of our lives. He has written each person's life to reveal His story. There never has been, nor ever will be, another life like mine—or yours. Just as there is only one face and name like mine, so there is only one story like mine. And the story of my life is written to make something known about the God who wrote me. The same is true of you. Your life and mine not only reveal who we are, they also help reveal who God is.[5]

Rex Miller tells us in his book *The Millennium Matrix* that today's generation of young people want to hear our stories. He also says, "Narrative and story, the ancient art of storytelling"[6] is growing as a means of communicating the gospel. God can always guide you to a place in your story that connects with another person and allows you to invite them to join you on this spiritual journey.

It only takes a short time to guide women through the process of explaining how Christ entered their personal world. All you need is a piece of paper and a pen. Divide the paper into three sections and title them "My Life before I Knew Christ," "How I Came to Know Christ," and "My Life Today with Christ." Women who came to know Christ at a young age might think their story is too simple or even boring, but their experience has now become the *unique* story and one that will amaze many nonbelievers. Encourage them to see it as a special gift from God and to share it freely.

As I grew in my understanding of sharing my faith, I discovered my own childhood experience had a universal connecting point—fear of death. I grew up attending church during an era of fire-and-brimstone messages. As a result, I was afraid of dying. I also remember turning out the light at night and feeling empty and lonely inside. One day I just called out to God through a very simple prayer: "Please forgive all my sins and come live in my life so I can live with you in heaven forever." The only thing I truly remember about that long-ago night is no longer feeling alone or afraid when I turned out the lights that night. In fact, I felt so full of God's love that I remember kicking off the sheets and spreading out my arms hoping to soak up more of it! I've never feared death since that time. I've also continued to feel Jesus Christ's love and presence through the past forty-six years. This simple story connects with every gender and every culture, and I've learned to share it as a way to connect with others. Write out your own experience with Christ, then challenge others to join you in doing the same.

Twelve women write daily devotionals to encourage Christian women and post them on their website, www.encouraging.com. They wanted to make sure anyone browsing the site had access to the gospel. Instead of writing out the basic facts of salvation, they decided to link their site to a seeker-sensitive interactive "gospel narrative" site designed specifically for women, www.journeyofjoy.com.[7] This site goes beyond sharing the gospel. It also offers four online Bible studies designed for new believers as well as assistance locating an evangelical church. It's also relational. Readers can browse other women's personal stories. Here's one example: "I believed that having children would bring me contentment, but as much as I loved my children, marriage and motherhood were not bringing the fulfillment I had longed for." I encourage you to visit this site and review these testimonies. Each offers a good example of how a personal story can provide an opportunity for another person to establish a saving relationship with Jesus Christ.

Reaching beyond Church Walls

Women often flinch at the thought of offending someone with the gospel. The website www.Nooma.com offers an effective downloadable video clip that provides a discussion starter for women. It's called "Bullhorn."[8] You'll find it under Nooma's Discussion Books. The producers draw us to the conclusion that we should do all things in love, just as Jesus commands us. Scripture also exhorts us to be light to a dark world. Opportunities abound, but working out the logistics requires intentional planning. Several years ago our church participated in a "love your neighbor" emphasis. Our pastor asked each member to reach out to someone with an act of kindness coupled with a prayer of God's blessing and an opportunity to share the gospel. The women responded eagerly to the challenge. Some ran errands for neighbors, wrote notes, babysat, baked, and made personal visits. I decided I'd take newspapers to the front doors of homes on my early morning walking route. At each home, I'd ask God to work in their lives in a special way that day. I prayed that the ones who knew him would remember his constant care and love. For those who didn't know him, I prayed that the Holy Spirit would continue to draw them to himself.

One church in Canada used acts of kindness as their number one strategy for making the church's presence known in the community. For a whole year the women brought home-baked cookies to break rooms at the fire department and hospital. They included note cards with the church's name with "Thank you for your service to the community. If we can be of help to you in any way, please call us." The outreach required organization and the women's commitment. It also produced results as community members began to take note and seek out the love of Christ.

Offering conversational English classes to international women provides a platform to build relationships with minority women in the community. All it takes is one woman with a passion to reach international women for Christ. The medical, academic, and business communities often bring in students and employees from other countries. Their wives are often isolated by the language and culture. These women enjoy the opportunity to make friends and to learn simple English. The personal time student and teacher spend together lays a foundation for sharing the Christian faith.

You'll find Christians involved in many areas of community service: food banks, pro-life clinics, Salvation Army,[9] Meals on Wheels,[10] soup kitchens, clothes closets, community day-care centers, prison ministries, nursing homes, and retirement homes. Just imagine the eternal gains if these volunteers consciously looked for opportunities to share their personal story. As leaders, we can remind and equip those we lead to remember why they serve others—to be conduits of Christ's saving grace.

Many churches have discovered self-contained mission fields in apartment complexes. Women work with the children through after-school activities. In the process, they begin building relationships with the mothers. One group of women hosts apartment laundromat outreaches. They advertise the day and time they'll be in the laundry room, then arrive with cold drinks, quarters, and detergent. They enjoy visiting with the women while the washers wash and the dryers tumble—always looking for an opportunity to share the cleansing power of Christ!

Sharing Christ Cross-culturally

I remember the wide eyes of high school students in China and in the former Eastern Germany as the mission team discussed the "American melting pot." Both groups of students had grown up in cultures priding themselves in ethnic purity. Americans have many sources of ethnic heritage. My own children have Scotch-Irish, German, Chocktaw American Indian, Polish, and Lithuanian heritage. What a paradox—we pride ourselves in our heritage, yet still seem to struggle with assimilating new ethnic minorities within our communities. Eight years ago, several women asked about hosting a Saturday morning conference for the women attending a nearby Hispanic mission. Thirty-two nervous women arrived with eyes cast downward and husbands in tow. The men waited patiently on the sofas throughout the conference while our teenage girls' mission group cared for the children in an adjacent room. We served coffee, sweets, and orange juice for breakfast and sandwiches, chips, and Coke for lunch. Both the simple food and teaching format transformed the downcast faces into radiant smiles, hugs, and tears by the time the women left five hours later. We also handed out pamphlets in Spanish that explained the saving love of Christ for the women to share with their friends. Each year the conference continues to grow and now includes breakout sessions for younger women. This year we're even offering breakout sessions for leadership development.

For several years I've had a desire to reach out to Muslim women. I prayed for the Lord to bring a Muslim woman into my life, and he answered my prayers beyond what I could even imagine. I had the opportunity to travel with a teammate into the heart of three Muslim countries to visit Christian historical sites, to pray, and to look for opportunities to meet Muslim women. Our eagerness to share what we'd learned on the trip led us to offer a three-part series we called "Befriending the Muslim Woman." We expected ten to fifteen women to attend, and fifty showed up! Women came for a variety of reasons. One attendee wanted to learn how to befriend the mother of her daughter's Muslim classmate. Another had a son in the military stationed in a Muslim country. Another woman had just accepted a job in London and hoped to live in a Muslim neighborhood where she could build relationships. One young woman attended a local college and felt called to reach Muslim students for Christ. Many just wanted to learn more about what Muslims believe. We later rejoiced to learn that two women began conversational English classes at the local mosque and are building rich friendships with the women.

Reaching the Marketplace

Look for ways to equip the marketplace women in your church to intentionally pray for their colleagues, to utilize friendship evangelism strategies, and to share their personal stories. The authors of *The Fourth Frontier*[11] believe that instead of seeing work as a negative that keeps us from spending time on truly important things, we should see it as a significant and critical part of our day. Relating our personal faith at work and with colleagues should be as much a part of our spiritual walk as Sunday mornings. They believe Christians should seek to experience a seamless connection between Friday and Sunday and between Sunday and Monday.

I enjoyed the flexibility of a part-time job and remaining home with my four children. When the youngest reached third grade, circumstances dictated I return to work full-time. I remember dropping off my son at school, then crying all the way to work. I'd pull up at the elementary school where I taught, dry my eyes, and wave to the jolly little crossing guard. I'd then take a deep breath and walk through the school's front door to face the day. By the end of the second year, I'd begun to realize God actually wanted me in that classroom and had allowed the circumstances to place me there. Once I understood that I was heading out on God's assignment each morning rather than just off to work, my attitude totally changed. I began to look for each day's opportunity to express God's love through words of encouragement or through prayer for those around me. I also prayed for my students and tried extra hard to invest in their lives. I personally experienced the transformation of a woman who sees her circumstances from God's perspective. It's the message we as leaders must communicate to each woman under our influence—trust that God has you where he needs you to serve him today.

Locating Evangelistic Resources

Do you wince at the thought of handing a woman an evangelistic tract? I did, but not any longer. Tracts are excellent tools to supplement your personal story or to leave with someone when you don't have an extended time to visit. Be sure it's women-friendly. Men want just the facts, but most women respond to information that's personal and sensitive. If you can't find what you're looking for, consider writing your own. The American Tract Society[12] online actually guides you through writing one.

Encourage the women to keep tracts in their purses or cars. Whenever the Holy Spirit nudges, offer one to a store employee on break or to the one who checks you out. I usually say something like, "Here's some reading for your next break," or "Here is something that means a lot to me personally. I hope you'll take time to read through it on your next break." Encourage the women to keep tracts in languages common to your area. They're an excellent way to cross language barriers when there's no interpreter.

Christianity Today sponsors a website called Outreach that challenges women to look for new ways to reach the twenty-first-century woman with the good news of God's love. You can explore creative resources at http://www.christianitytoday.com/outreach/features/targeted-women.html. I'm particularly amazed by the concept of a digital tract you can send by email.[13]

Outreach magazine[14] offers monthly ideas and encouragement to share your faith with others. Visit their website at www.outreachmagazine.com and search the women's category for ideas for effectively communicating the gospel. You'll also want to consider Marilyn Meberg's excellent evangelistic booklet for women called *The Decision of a Lifetime*.[15] It focuses on God choosing us and adopting us into his family.

Children and students originally began using bracelets with colored beads to share the gospel with their friends. You can use this same concept in women's jewelry, both costume jewelry with plastic beads and sterling silver bracelets with fine stones. Someone's comment provides an opportunity to explain the symbolic meaning of each colored stone: black for man's sin, red for Christ's blood, white for a cleansed life, blue for eternity, and green for spiritual growth. Teams of all ages enjoy a resource called Evangecube.[16] It's a series of cubes joined together in such a way that you can open it from different angles. The pictures tell the complete gospel story. I'm just amazed every time I pick one up. They come in all sizes, including key-ring size. They're fun to use and effective!

Encourage women to share their faith in whatever way fits their personality and fits the situation. It builds the kingdom of God and makes an eternal difference in another's life. As God creates an evangelistic heart within you, it will ripple through those you lead. Together you'll move forward in response to the biblical directive to "shine like stars in the universe as you hold out the word of life" (Phil. 2:15–16).

For Reflection

1. Every believer has a responsibility to pass on the message of God's salvation. Describe the last time you shared the good news of Christ's saving love with someone.

2. Learning to pray evangelistically is a good way to ease hesitant women into reaching friends and family for Christ. What does the phrase "evangelistic praying" mean to you? Name those you're currently praying for.

3. Women often flinch at the thought of offending someone with the gospel. What are some women-friendly approaches to sharing Christ?

4. Look for ways to equip the marketplace women in your church to intentionally pray for their colleagues, to utilize friendship evangelism strategies, and to share their personal stories. Describe someone you know who is already doing these things.

17

EQUIPPING AND SENDING

As you sent me into the world,
I have sent them into the world.

John 17:18

SHERRY WALLACE

Sherry (not her real name) listened as the guest speaker spoke of the need for Christian workers in countries closed to the gospel. Her heart warmed as she thought of actually going to one of those places. Sherry had always enjoyed reading stories of women who served God in distant places, and her mother had taught her to pray for those who went. Now God was actually calling her to go. She began raising her support to teach English in China through the English Language Institute,[1] a Christian organization registered with the Chinese government to provide English teachers for their universities. By the second year, Sherry's support had dwindled, and she wondered if she'd be able to continue her work overseas. During a visit home, her church's women's ministry helped set up speaking opportunities to tell women about her work. Many committed to be a part of her prayer and financial support team. Today Sherry's enjoying her sixth year of serving Christ in China.

Equipping and sending are foundational functions of the church. Involving women in a mission trip impacts their lives, the church, and the kingdom. A women's ministry that equips and sends short-term women's teams or even full-time workers must nurture a missions awareness by consistently exposing women to the needs and opportunities in the world. Involvement in missions includes both the one who goes and those who financially or prayerfully support the worker from home. By providing a variety of opportunities to participate in missions, women's ministry leaders obey Jesus's admonition recorded in Matthew 9:38 to "ask the Lord of the harvest . . . to send out workers to his harvest field."

Supporting through Prayer

Throughout the history of the church, women have supported in prayer those who leave the local church to serve in other countries. Today's leaders have many ways to challenge women to continue that vital prayer support. Pam Thedford provides passionate leadership for equipping others in prayer. She and a group of women are always ready to intercede. She also contagiously shares her joy of prayer with others through facilitating studies on prayer. Pam challenges women to begin praying "out of the boat," praying for things that require more faith than the security of practical prayers—trusting God for big things. We pray "out of the boat" when we intercede for those serving in very difficult locations. These families face the ongoing challenges of spiritual warfare, sickness, isolation, cultural challenges, and complicated logistics of daily necessities as they seek to share the good news of Christ's death, burial, and resurrection. We catch Paul's missionary heart when he wrote to the Christians in Thessalonica, saying, "We lived among you for your sake. . . . We were gentle among you, like a mother caring for her little children. We loved you so much that we were delighted to share with you not only the gospel of God but our lives as well, because you had become so dear to us" (1 Thess. 1:5; 2:7–8).

Supporting through Giving

Women have given financial support to God's work from the earliest days of Christ's ministry. We read about it in Luke 8:1–4. Luke recorded that Mary Magdalene, Susanna, and Joanna helped to support Jesus and the disciples out of their own means. Women tend to give spontaneously, responding joyfully to specific needs. As a woman in leadership, you have the opportunity and responsibility to encourage and model joyful giving. Be supportive if your church has a specific missions-giving emphasis. Make sure the women have the information they need so they can be informed givers.

Encourage women to investigate another option for financially supporting missions—purchasing handcrafted items made by indigenous women. Women can access products online[2] or through catalogs.[3] Your leadership team might also consider sending a woman on a missions assignment supported both financially and prayerfully by the women of the church. It's a wonderful way to be a part of God's work, just like Mary Magdalene, Joanna, and Susanna. Be sensitive to other mission opportunities God might lay on your heart, and share them with the women. Always check with your pastor first to make sure the opportunities are in line with the goals of the church.

Sending Teams

Discerning God's design for a women's mission team requires prayer, research, and planning. *The Essential Guide to the Short Term Mission Trip* by David Forward reminds us that "Christians are better educated, more globally conscious, and more technically equipped to take the Gospel to unchurched and unreached people groups than ever before."[4] We have more reasons to go than ever before. Check with your denominational or evangelical organizations for training manuals and other useful resources as you pray and plan. It's also helpful to consult with someone who has actually made that specific trip or a similar trip.

Investigate places your church currently works and look for ways to participate. Women's ministry might consider teaching the mothers and grandmothers while the church or youth team works with children in Bible school activities. Several years ago our high school girls' mission group traveled to El Paso to host a children's Bible club in a city park. Women's ministry sent a Spanish-speaking woman to teach Bible classes to the mothers while the girls taught the children. On the last day, the kids hugged and smiled as they said goodbye, but the mothers said goodbye with hugs and tears.

If the team works on location with a specific church, consider ways to invest quality time with the local pastor's wife during the team's stay. Check to see what resources she needs and take them with you. If several churches work together with your team, consider gathering the pastors' wives for a special conference. These women often work so hard, they never get to enjoy the fellowship of one another.

Considering More Options

I received an email from a mother sharing stories from a recent mother-daughter mission trip. The team went to many different locations to pray for those who walked past them. She said, "The girls particularly enjoyed interacting with children and students. I was blessed to see my shy daughter actually talking about Jesus with the young people on the city square." I immediately forwarded the email to our leadership team and asked them to pray about sponsoring our own mother-daughter trip. Jennifer Paul provides leadership for our missions focus and has already begun investigating options for a trip next year, complete with mother-daughter fund-raisers. It'll be our first, and I can't wait to see how God brings all the details together.

I heard another women-friendly mission idea from a worker in a country closed to the gospel. She called it "blitzing." Team members enter the country as tourists and just do ordinary tourist activities, including shopping and eating out. When they're shopping, though, they leave Christian literature in the pockets of the clothes they try on or in the dressing rooms. They discreetly leave literature in seats of taxis and restaurant restrooms—anywhere someone will find it after they're gone. This is a powerful outreach when coupled with prayer for each person who reads the information. They leave the fruit of this strategy totally in God's hands. Only in eternity will they know how God used their efforts to increase his kingdom.

The universal language of music offers limitless avenues of sharing God's love. Even when listeners don't understand the lyrics, they see the radiance of those who sing. Ensembles on city squares always draw a crowd. They can offer gospel tracks in the local language, a warm smile, and a silent prayer for each person receiving it. Not every team member needs to have musical abilities. Teams always need intercessors and those who provide support for the performers. Visit orphanages and share children's songs and hand games. Pray that God would protect those little ones and provide loving Christian homes.

The U.S. and Canada still wrestle with the cultural needs of the Native North Americans. Christians especially have something to offer: God's love. I remember walking into a basement classroom of an evangelical seminary outside of Calgary in Alberta, Canada. I stood transfixed by what I saw—twelve sewing machines and piles of fabric. Multiple sets of children's clothes hung from hooks around all four sides of the room. The activity immediately drew me in. The women sewed clothing for children on a nearby Indian reservation. These families were not receptive to summer Bible school activities for their children, but they did accept clothing. Labels sewn inside each item relayed the message, "Jesus loves you." The women's laughter and joy warmed my heart, and their sewing skills spread God's love to little children.

Medical missions share God's love by meeting basic needs. Women from your church can participate in medical missions by joining a medical team in ministry or by teaching hygiene and personal health care to women while they wait in line to receive medical care. I'll never forget Kalina's colorful story after participating on a dental mission trip along the Amazon River. While the mothers and children waited in lines, she watched one mother walk to the muddy river to wet a dirty rag. She then proceeded wiping the matted eyes and runny noses of all the children in line—with the same rag. Kalina instantly saw an opportunity for teaching some very basic hygiene to the women in this village.

Praying On-site

I vividly remember thumbing through a mission-focused magazine and stopping to study a picture of a gray-haired lady in a small boat. The caption read "Prayer Walking in India." I read and reread the article, trying to grasp a new concept of praying. I still remember the gripping impact that picture had on me. I tore the article out of the magazine and placed it in my "prayer" file. From that moment on, I had a desire to participate in something as amazing as praying on location in countries that do not know of Christ's love.

Several years later I had my first opportunity to participate in a mission trip with prayer as the focus. I actually phoned the lady in the picture to ask a very key question: "Is there a special strategy for doing what you did in India?" I still smile when I reflect on her answer. She said, "Honey, you just pray. You pray wherever you are." That's really all she had to say. I've since discovered resources[5] with suggestions and Scriptures for praying "on-site," but the basics remain the same, simply praying as the Holy Spirit leads you to pray.

Over the years I've had the privilege of prayer walking, prayer driving, prayer flying, and prayer sitting in countries and places I never even had faith to ask to visit: Mexico, Belize, China, Argentina, Germany, Cuba, Algeria, Tunisia, Jordon, Israel, and Canada. I've prayed that the Holy Spirit would draw the hearts of individuals that passed by while I sat in parks, peered out bus windows, stood on hilltops, walked crowded streets, and looked down upon alleys from hotel windows. Can you pray without going on location? Yes, certainly, but praying on location provides special insight. Steve Hawthorne calls it "praying on-site with insight."[6] Randy Sprinkle calls *prayer-walking* "in-the-world-intercession."[7] There's no doubt that the prayers stirred within my heart on location are quite different from the ones I pray from my kitchen table. Looking into a woman's eyes and seeing despair, hearing city or countryside sounds, and smelling the local food heightens your senses. You're able to pray for the child peeking at you from behind her mother's skirt instead of praying for children in general. You pray for the woman spooning your soup rather than for the women of China. Both types of praying are a privilege and responsibility, but women in leadership have an opportunity to nurture kingdom intercessors by going together on location and interceding.

Providing Spiritual Preparation

Prepare team members for spiritual warfare. Satan does not want the trip to happen and works to discourage team members from going. If women expect the unexpected, they're less discouraged when it does happen. Also, enlist a prayer support team and pray for one another consistently leading up to the trip, during the trip, and in the days following the trip. Having a specific Bible study for the women to experience together also helps build team unity. Paul asked the Christians in Thessalonica to

> pray for us that the message of the Lord may spread rapidly and be honored, just as it was with you. And pray that we may be delivered from wicked and evil men, for not everyone has faith. But the Lord is faithful, and he will strengthen and protect you from the evil one.
>
> 2 Thessalonians 3:1–3

I love what I read in a commentary concerning this passage:

> The apostles acknowledged the success of their missionary labors was due to God's blessing His Word as they proclaimed it. In particular, the spreading of the gospel was God's work and its reception among those who heard it was due to His preparing their hearts. The Thessalonians knew from their experiences how God works in people's hearts to prepare them to receive the gospel; so they could pray with conviction that God would honor His Word by causing others who heard it to believe it.[8]

What a wonderfully refreshing reminder— go, then leave it all in God's hands!

For Reflection

1. A women's ministry that equips and sends short-term women's teams or even full-time workers must consistently expose women to needs and opportunities in the world. Through what avenues do women in your church receive this type of information?

2. Throughout the history of the church, women have prayerfully supported those who serve Christ in other

countries. In what way are the women in your church encouraged to continue that vital prayer support?

3. A woman in leadership has the opportunity and responsibility of encouraging and modeling joyful giving. How do you see women's ministry supporting your church's mission giving emphasis?

4. Prepare team members for spiritual warfare. Satan will work to discourage team members from going. Describe your most recent encounter with spiritual warfare.

18

CONTAGIOUS DEVOTION

May he work in us what is pleasing to him
through Jesus Christ.

Hebrews 13:21

ALICE YOUNGBLOOD
AND LOIS BRAYMER

Alice and Lois shared a passion. They both wanted women to communicate to future generations through family stories illustrating godly character and devotion to God. After much planning, they decided to combine their skills as a librarian and an English teacher. They invited women to a twelve-week series where they wrote stories about family members to share with their children and grandchildren. Lois and Alice encouraged the women by guiding the writing and editing process. Each participant added a photograph to illustrate their story and stored their completed project in archival-quality protective sleeves. The women honored those who had spiritually influenced their lives by leaving written legacies to encourage future generations.

God wants our lives as Christians to encourage those who come behind us. Steve Green recorded a song that captures the heart of what God desires for all of his followers—including the women in your church. The lyrics form a simple yet powerful prayer:

May all who come behind us find us faithful.
May the fire of our devotion light their way.
May the footprints that we leave
Lead them to believe
And the lives we live inspire them to obey.

Does that sound like a lofty request? Does it stir your heart to think that God could use your own devotion to Christ to encourage faithfulness in those who come behind you? It's God's plan for all believers. Only he can accomplish this supernatural work, and he will if we let him.

Think of women in your own life who have influenced your spiritual development. Go back to your childhood, if possible, and search for those women whose consistency in their faith made your own world feel more secure. Whose devotion continues to light your way today? I think of Mae Shirey, a short woman with a steady-paced, childlike voice. I remember her consistent presence and her gentle ways. I also consider my precious little granny an example of a devoted life. As an adult, I understood the source of her strength, her faith, and her prayer life. As a child, I only knew she never said anything unkind about anyone. I knew her Bible had worn covers, and she never missed attending church. She also wanted her grandchildren with her at church on Easter Sunday—all lined up in the pew beside her.

Observing Devotion

My life continues to be significantly impacted by the women who remained with Christ throughout the horrors of the crucifixion, through the darkness, and even through the earthquake. What was the source of their devotion? It was the same source that we have, a relationship with Jesus

Christ who forgives sin and sets us free to love and adore him. He walks with us and talks with us. He shares our sorrows and the trials we face in a sin-filled world. Those women's devotion continues to light my way today. They're some of the first people I plan on seeking when I reach heaven!

Asaph, one of King David's musicians, wrote the lyrics in Psalm 78. His psalm is listed as a *maskil*, a song of instruction. The words remind us to tell our children how God has worked in our lives. Doing so encourages their faithfulness to the Lord: "Tell the next generation the praiseworthy deeds of the LORD, his power, and the wonders he has done" (v. 4). Our forefathers taught God's laws to their children "so the next generation would know them, even the children yet to be born, and they in turn would tell their children. Then they would put their trust in God and would not forget his deeds but would keep his commands" (vv. 6–7).

The structure of women's ministry facilitates this generational storytelling. We study God's Word and share with one another how God is using it in our lives. Moms share these same truths with their children who grow up telling their children about God's grace and provision in their lives. This process has continued since Mary Magdalene and the women with her told the disciples, "The tomb is empty!" Believers today from around the world keep on telling the stories of these earliest eyewitnesses to Christ's ministry. You have the opportunity to inspire women to look for opportunities to communicate timeless truths in their generation.

My youngest daughter recently presented to me a Bible dated 1843 for Mother's Day. Its fragile pages contain records of the original owners' marriage as well as births and deaths of their five children. I have no idea when the Bible became lost to the couple's descendants. Was it misplaced or was it sold because no one valued the faith of their ancestors? Even though individual family histories might come and go, the church family remains constant. No matter how far away you move, you can always find an extended church family with whom you can share your stories of God's faithfulness.

Praying for Future Devotion

Jennifer Kennedy Dean believes in the influence of prayer for future generations. She writes in *Legacy of Prayer*, "We can leave behind for our descendants a spiritual trust that can never be stolen, squandered, or lost. We can leave riches that will only increase in value. We can lay up a store of imperishable wealth."[1] Before I even knew the names and faces of my own children, I desired to live a devoted life to God before them. I felt such inadequacy I remember asking my grandmother to begin storing up prayers for me right then—so I'd experience the results long after she was gone. In addition, I asked her to pray for my children, even before they were conceived. I didn't even know at the time if those were valid requests. I'm so glad I did! Jesus prayed for us long before we came to know him. As he prayed for his disciples in John 17:15–21, he included us: "My prayer is not for them alone. I pray also for those who will believe in me through their message, that all of them may be one, Father, just as you are in me and I am in you."

We ought also to pray for the women who will come after us. Pray for devoted lives, single-minded lives, and lives of purity. Pray that God would sanctify and equip them in his Word in preparation for leadership responsibilities. Pray they will dream God's dreams for his church and for the women who serve there. Pray for their singleness or for their marriage and family responsibilities. Pray that the Holy Spirit will sanctify and empower their lives. Pray also that God will continue to spread the good news of his salvation through them.

My sister, Claudia, sketched a picture for me. The picture began with a small group of women in the distance near the cross of Christ and continued with a long line of women winding forward, around hills and valleys continuing right up to today. It perfectly caught on paper what I felt about those women who have gone before us. The second verse of the song "Find Us Faithful"[2] communicates the same idea:

> But as those who've gone before us,
> Let us leave to those behind us
> The heritage of faithfulness
> Passed on through godly lives.

As women extend their hand to one woman and the next and the next, the stories of God's strength and his wonderful works encourage others to put their confidence in God and keep his commandments.

Accepting the Challenge

If we live our own lives devoted to the Christ who loved us enough to die for us, then God will accomplish the inevitable—the fires of our devotion will light the way for those women who come after us. Let's intentionally look for ways to pass on what God has taught us. Then, let's encourage those who come behind us to do the same. The author of Hebrews penned the perfect benediction for us when he wrote:

> May the God of peace, who through the blood of the eternal covenant brought back from the dead our Lord Jesus, that great Shepherd of the sheep, equip you with everything good for doing his will, and may he work in us what is pleasing to him, through Jesus Christ, to whom be glory forever. Amen.
>
> Hebrews 13:20–21

For Reflection

1. Reflect on those women whose consistency in their faith made your own world feel more secure. Whose devotion continues to light your way today?

2. The structure of women's ministry facilitates this generational storytelling through small group Bible studies. As we study God's Word, we share with one another how God is using it in our lives. What other generational encouragement opportunities would you like to see available in your church?

3. Moms share biblical truths with their children who grow up telling their children about God's grace and provision in their lives. How many generations back can you trace a Christian legacy in your life?

4. If we live our lives devoted to the one who died for us, then God will accomplish the inevitable—the fires of our devotion will light the way for women who come after us. Take time to ask God to accomplish this through your own life.

Appendix 1

Understanding a Saving Relationship with Christ

My husband spent the first eighteen years of his life worshiping and learning about God. He had no doubts that Jesus was born as a baby to Mary and was crucified as a sacrifice for our sin. Yet this knowledge of God did not satisfy or make a difference in his life. He smiles as he reflects on a pretty blonde girl who invited him to a skating party. Round and round they went until suddenly the light came on, the music stopped, and everyone sat down on the skating rink floor. A guy with a guitar appeared and talked about the difference a personal relationship with Christ had made in his life. Later this same attractive blonde invited him to a crusade in downtown Chicago where Tom Skinner, a converted New York gang member, spoke. Some months later, a student walked up to Gary in the student center of the University of Chicago. He asked if he could read through a small booklet presenting a simple plan of salvation: (1) Man is sinful. (2) Jesus died for our sin. (3) We must accept this gift of salvation for ourselves. (4) You can accept this gift by acknowledging you are a sinner and by asking Jesus to forgive your sins.

Gary realized what he needed to do. Silently, he prayed, "Lord Jesus, I know I am a sinner. Please forgive my sins. Come into my life and be Lord of my life." That moment became a pivotal point in Gary's life. The empty longing inside disappeared, and a personal relationship with Christ began that continues to grow to this day, thirty-eight years later.

If you feel longing inside and can't recall talking personally to God about accepting this gift of salvation, then take time to speak with him now. Simply tell him how you're feeling. If you need to, ask him to help you find the words. John 3:16 is one of the first verses taught to children:

> For God so loved the world that he gave his one and only Son, that whoever believes in him shall not perish but have eternal life.

The Greek word for "believe" means "placing your confidence in," much like sitting down in a chair demonstrates you have confidence it will hold you up. You can express this belief through prayer. You can pray something similar to what Gary prayed: "Lord Jesus, I believe you died for my sins. Please forgive my independent and sinful ways and be Lord of my life." Take time to pause and pray right now. His love will begin to flood the tiniest lonely spots in your soul and bring light where shadows once dwelt.

Appendix 2

Leadership Team Member Guidelines*

George Barna defines a *leadership team* as a small group of leaders who have complementary gifts and skills and who are committed to each other's growth and success while leading a larger group of people in a pursuit of a common vision. Team members have three dominant characteristics: They are all leaders. Their gifts complement each other. And they have a passion for the same vision. With this profile of a team and team members in mind, it's easy to see the requirements needed for membership on the leadership team:

Team members are leaders called by God.

They have character that honors God.

They possess competencies to get the job done.

*George Barna, *The Power of Team Leadership: Achieving Success through Shared Responsibility* (Colorado Springs: WaterBrook, 2001). Used by permission.

They are trustworthy.

They demonstrate team priorities rather than individual priorities.

They make meaningful contributions to the team but not necessarily equal contributions.

They are highly disciplined and diligent.

They are willing to study and learn.

They demonstrate proper priorities.

APPENDIX 3

WHY HAVE A WOMEN'S ENRICHMENT MINISTRY?

WOMEN'S MINISTRY PLANNING GUIDE

1. To help churches grow numerically and spiritually.
2. To help women feel accepted when they join your church.
3. To open the door to meaningful relationships.
4. To encourage women to discover, develop, and use their spiritual gifts.
5. To minister to today's women.
6. To provide vision and networking for both inreach and outreach ministries.
7. To offer "woman-to-woman" understanding.
8. To offer "woman-to-woman" lay counseling.
9. To encourage spiritually older women to mentor (teach) spiritually younger women.

10. To follow Jesus's example of ministry to and with women.
11. To help women fight spiritual battles.
12. To affect families as women's lives are drawn closer to Christ.

"Women's Ministry Planning Guide 2006," Promo #B845C99, LifeWay Church Resources. Reprinted and used by permission.

Appendix 4

Women's Ministry Survey

The women of the church would like to hear from you as they plan for the coming year.

1. What would you consider to be most important to you?
   - ☐ Bible study
   - ☐ Discipleship
   - ☐ Ministry opportunities
   - ☐ Prayer
   - ☐ Fellowship

2. What times would you prefer for a Bible study?
   - ☐ Weekday
   - ☐ Sunday evening
   - ☐ Wednesday evening
   - ☐ Saturday morning
   - ☐ Other _____

3. What topics interest you most?
   - ☐ Topical study
   - ☐ Book of the Bible
   - ☐ Marriage
   - ☐ Parenting
   - ☐ Preferred author _____

4. What length of study do you prefer?
   - ☐ 4 weeks
   - ☐ 6 weeks
   - ☐ 8 weeks
   - ☐ 10 weeks
   - ☐ 12 weeks

5. What length of "homework" do you prefer?
   - ☐ none
   - ☐ 30 minutes/day
   - ☐ 1 hour/day
   - ☐ Other _____

6. Would you need childcare?
   - ☐ Yes   ☐ No

7. Have you had experience in facilitating a small group Bible study?
   - ☐ Yes   ☐ No

8. Would you be willing to facilitate a study?
   - ☐ Yes   ☐ No
   - ☐ Will pray about it

9. What activity would you participate in?
   - ☐ Retreat
   - ☐ Conference
   - ☐ Luncheon
   - ☐ Ministry project
   - ☐ Mission trip

10. Are you available to assist with leadership in any of these areas?
    - ☐ Yes   ☐ No

    If "yes," which area(s)? _____

Name: _____

Address: _____

_____

Cell phone: _____

Home phone: _____

Email: _____

APPENDIX 5

LIFE EXPERIENCES INVENTORY

SHARING GOD'S COMFORT

Occasionally, life feels overwhelming and we struggle to find the comfort, encouragement, and hope for the future that Christ offers. That's when the body of Christ has an opportunity to demonstrate Christ's tender compassion and encouragement to one another.

Prayerfully ask God to guide you as you read through the attached Life Experiences Inventory. Seek to know which ones he wants you to share with another woman needing comfort and hope.

Circle the items. Mail or return the inventory to the women's ministry office. Inventories will be stored in a secure and confidential file. Should another woman desire to speak with someone who understands her situation, we will contact you. You will then be asked to give her a call. Your name and phone number will not be given to anyone.

If you've had experiences that you are not ready to share, we encourage you to continue seeking God's healing. He's ready and waiting to move you forward and into a new season of acceptance and forgiveness, comfort and hope.

Praise be to the God and Father of our Lord Jesus Christ, the Father of compassion and the God of all comfort, who comforts us in all our troubles, so that we can comfort those in any trouble with the comfort we ourselves have received from God. For just as the sufferings of Christ flow over into our lives, so also through Christ our comfort overflows.

2 Corinthians 1:3–5

∽∂⃝ ⃝∂∾

Life Experiences Inventory

Circle any life experience you are willing to share with another woman.

Abortion
(self) (child) (grandchild)
Abuse (verbal, physical)
Adoption
(adults seeking birth parents)
(adults desiring to adopt)
(placed a child up for adoption)
Adult child of an alcoholic parent
Adultery
AIDS in a family member
Alcohol addiction
Anger issues
(self) (spouse)
Attention Deficit Disorder (ADD)
(child) (spouse) (self)
Autistic child

222

Bankruptcy
Bipolar disorder
  (self) (spouse) (child)
Breast cancer
Caregiver for elderly parent
Chemical dependency
  (self) (spouse) (child)
Chronic pain
Codependency recovery
Death
  (infant) (child) (teenager) (parent)
Depression
  (self) (spouse) (child)
Dialysis
  (self) (family member)
Divorce
Domestic violence
  (self) (parents)
Eating disorders
  (anorexia) (bulemia)
Emotional affairs
Empty nest
Estranged adult child
Fibromyalgia
Financial loss
Homosexuality
  (self) (spouse) (child)
Hysterectomy
Infertility
Injured child
Job loss

Learning-disabled child
Marital conflicts
Mastectomy/reconstructive surgery
Mentally handicapped child
Miscarriage
Multiple sclerosis
Physically handicapped child
PMS
Pornography addiction
    (self) (spouse) (child)
Prescription drug abuse/addiction
    (self) (family member)
Rape
    (self) (child)
Schizophrenia
    (child) (family member)
Sexual abuse
    (self) (child)
Suicide of a family member
    (child) (adult) (spouse) (parent)
Unplanned pregnancy
Weight loss
Widowhood

Other: _____

_____

_____

Name: _____

Phone: _____

Email: _____

APPENDIX 6

LEADING THROUGH THE POWER OF THE HOLY SPIRIT

Leaders must depend upon the Holy Spirit if they want the results of their leadership to bring glory to God. Jesus made provision for the disciples and those who came after them, saying, "I will ask the Father, and he will give you another counselor to be with you forever—the Spirit of Truth" (John 14:16–17). The Holy Spirit indwells believers (John 5–6) and fills believers who yield in obedience to God's command to be filled (Eph. 5:18).

Look to the Holy Spirit to:

Conquer Sin

A life continually yielded to the control of the Spirit results in personal victory over sin (Eph. 4:30). Crucifying by faith our sinful nature with its passions and desires allows us to "live by the Spirit" and to "keep in step with the Spirit" (Gal. 5:25).

Reveal God's Word

Look to the Holy Spirit when studying God's Word, because as the Spirit of truth, he will guide you into all truth. The Spirit will take God's truth and give you the ability to understand it (John 16:13–15). Jesus described the work of the Holy Spirit to the disciples in John 14:26: "The Counselor, the Holy Spirit, whom the Father will send in my name, will teach you all things and will remind you of everything I have said to you." Look also to the Holy Spirit to lead you as you make decisions about life and about leadership responsibilities (Rom. 8:14).

Guide You in Prayer

When you pray, do as Paul instructed: "Pray in the Spirit on all occasions with all kinds of prayers and requests" (Eph. 6:18). When you don't know how to pray, seek the Holy Spirit who "helps us in our weakness. . . . because the Spirit intercedes for the saints in accordance with God's will" (Rom. 8:26–27).

Take the Offensive in Spiritual Warfare

When you stand against the devil's schemes, "stand firm" but take the offensive with the "sword of the Spirit, which is the word of God" (Eph. 6:14–17).

Empower Spiritual Gifts

Look to the Holy Spirit to empower you in understanding and developing your spiritual gifts. "Now to each one the manifestation of the Spirit is given for the common good. . . . All these are the work of one and the same Spirit, and he gives them to each one, just as he determines" (1 Cor. 12:7, 11).

Produce Fruit

As leaders, we must depend on the Holy Spirit to express his characteristics or "fruit" (defined as love, joy, peace, patience, kindness, goodness, faithfulness, gentleness, and self-control) rather than attempting to find these qualities from within ourselves (Gal. 5:22–23).

APPENDIX 7

SPIRITUAL GIFTS

Understanding the role of spiritual gifts empowers a woman to serve because she has the confidence God has specifically equipped her for ministry through her life experiences, her calling, and her spiritual gift. It's important for you as a leader to guide women to serve in the power of the Holy Spirit and in the areas of their giftedness.

You'll discover a wide variety of perspectives on the subject of spiritual gifts, even within the same denomination. Deciding on the specific resource to use for leadership purposes will require prayerful discernment. You'll also want to check with your church leadership for suggestions. For the purposes of *Connecting Women*, we'll focus on the point that most Christians agree on—that all believers have a spiritual gift: "To each one the manifestation of the Spirit is given for the common good" (1 Cor. 12:7).

The Bible discusses spiritual gifts in four key passages: Romans 12, Ephesians 4, 1 Corinthians 12–14, and 1 Peter 4. It's important to note that Scripture does not actually provide a definition of each of these gifts other than the meanings of the Greek words. In 1 Peter 4:10–11, we see spiritual gifts divided into two broad categories, speaking and serving. Helping women identify their gift in one of these two areas provides a relatively easy starting point. You can also readily discern strengths in one of these two areas as you observe women. I've included a unique inventory based on a very simple premise: Spiritual gifts are an expression of the Holy Spirit living within you. The characteristic of the Holy Spirit that you're particularly drawn to just might be the gift he's given to you. An inventory can be a helpful tool, but must be considered just that—a tool. Intellectual exercises will never replace discovery through doing.

John Bisagno, former pastor of First Baptist Church, Houston, once summarized a message on spiritual gifts by saying, "Whatever you do well, do!" I'd like to add, though, that using your gift brings joy. So, *my* concluding statement is, "Do whatever you like to do and whatever it is you do well—all to the glory of God!"

∞∞

The Holy Spirit,
His Characteristics and Activities Inventory

Directions: Circle two items listed below describing a work or a characteristic of the Holy Spirit you consider most important in your life. Then check the matching spiritual gifts and their descriptions that follow.

1. Frees us from the power of sin (Rom. 8:1–2; 2 Thess. 2:13).

2. Provides leadership to individuals (Acts 8:29); helps us plan and organize his work (1 Chron. 28:12).

3. Convicts the world of sin (John 16:8); leads non-Christians to confess that Jesus is Lord (1 Cor. 12:3); brings a person to new life in Christ (John 3:5–6).

4. Empowers us to speak with conviction and boldness (Acts 2:4, 14–18).

5. Offers guidance to the church in its administration (Acts 13:2).

6. Comforts us (John 14:16).

7. Appoints us to places of service in the church (Acts 20:28).

8. Stimulates the proper use of possessions within the Christian community (Acts 4:31–32).

9. Teaches us and reminds us of the things of God (John 14:26; 16:13; 1 Cor. 2:10–13).

10. Causes us to overflow with hope (Rom. 15:13) and reassures us we are children of God (Rom. 8:16–17).

11. Teaches and reveals the deep things of God and the mysteries of Christ (Eph. 3:3–6).

12. Empowers us to be a witness for Jesus Christ (Acts 1:8).

13. Understands our thoughts and intercedes for us (Rom. 8:26–27).

14. Provides counsel (John 14:26).

15. Empowers us to do God's will with an attitude of joy and peace (Rom. 14:17–18).

16. Gives gifts to men and women as he chooses (1 Cor. 12:4–7).

Now see which spiritual gifts correspond to the activities of the Holy Spirit with which you most closely identify:

229

Item Number	Spiritual Gifts
1 and 4	**Prophecy** declaring the purposes of God (Rom. 12:6)
2 and 5	**Administration** the governing of the duties of service (1 Cor. 12:28)
3 and 12	**Evangelism** announcing the good news of the gospel (Eph. 4:11)
6 and 13	**Mercy** compassionate help for someone afflicted or seeking aid (Rom. 12:8)
7 and 15	**Service or administration** the rendering of assistance (Rom. 12:7) or the governing of the duties of service (1 Cor. 12:28)
8 and 16	**Giving** imparting (Rom. 12:8)
9 and 11	**Teaching** explaining or instructing (Rom. 12:7)
10 and 14	**Exhortation** admonishing or encouraging (Rom. 12:8)

APPENDIX 8

MENTORING

Sample Mentoring Application

INTENTIONAL FRIENDS
MENTORING APPLICATION

Date: _____/_____/_____

Name: _____

Birth Date: ____/____/____ Age: ____

Address: _____

City: _____Zip: _____

Home Phone: _____

Email: _____

Occupation: _____

Business Phone: _____

Single/ Engaged/ Married (__ years)

Blended Family/ Divorced (__ years)

Widowed (__ years)

Children's Ages: _____

Grandchildren's Ages: _____

Stepchildren's Ages: _____
　　　　　Living with you?　☐ Yes　☐ No

Age I accepted Christ: _____

I want to be a: Mentor / Mentee / Either / Both

I'm interested in the following format for a mentoring relationship:

☐ Face-to-Face Friends　　☐ Email Mentoring
☐ Coffee Buddies　　　　　☐ Phone Mentoring
☐ Breakfast Buddies　　　　☐ Lunch Mates
☐ Walking Buddies

Is there anything in your life today that you feel would interfere with you being a mentor?

_____

_____

_____

_____

Hobbies, interests, gifts:

_____

_____

_____

_____

What I desire in this relationship is:

_____

_____

_____

_____

Please continue on the back and share any additional information you feel would be helpful in making an Intentional Friend match.

Sample Mentoring Evaluation

INTENTIONAL FRIENDS
EVALUATION

Rate your overall experience as a mentor:
- ☐ OK
- ☐ good
- ☐ excellent

Comments:

_____

_____

_____

_____

Would you want to serve as a mentor again?
- ☐ Yes ☐ No

Comments:

_____

_____

_____

_____

What was the highlight of your time as a mentor?

_____

_____

_____

_____

What was one of your frustrations as a mentor?

_____

_____

_____

_____

Would you be interested in mentoring through email?
☐ Yes ☐ No

Would you prefer more organized opportunities for you and your mentee to be together? yes no

Additional comments:

_____

_____

_____

_____

_____

Did this time frame work for you?
☐ Yes ☐ No

Do you have a preferred time frame?

_____

Name (optional) _____

APPENDIX 9

PERSONAL LEADERSHIP PRAYERS

I recently reviewed prayers I recorded and dated in the back of my Bible and my personal journal. I only recall the circumstances of a few. I do know they came as cries from the depth of my heart during challenging times. I dated them so I could later return to see how God answered them. I offer them as testimony to his faithfulness.

Lord, as I begin my new year at a new position of responsibility, I can't help but think how quiet my surroundings are. I'm used to halls of laughter and squeals, hordes of children heading to their classes. Help me get used to the quietness. But most of all, I pray for wisdom for the new responsibilities ahead. I love you. *1/4/95*

Father, my heart stirs to observe how Jesus ignored cultural influence of his day in how he related to women. Beyond entrusting himself to be born of a woman, he included them in his kingdom work. He sought out their homes for teaching and ministry, rest and renewal. He received both their prayer and financial support. He commissioned a woman with his message of salvation and with the most significant message of all time—*I have risen!*

I ask that this same Jesus who lives in hearts today will equip faithful men in positions of influence to not only see with your eyes and feel with your heart concerning women but also to join with you in facilitating your work among and through them.

May these men step boldly beyond the constraints of protocol and tradition to open doors, chart courses, and enable your mighty work of calling out faithful women to encourage and equip other women in your kingdom work . . . so that in your fullness of time, the work will be completed and you can gather both men and women to your throne where we will proclaim with one voice *Holy, Holy, Holy is the Lord God Almighty who was, and is, and is to come.* It's in the name of this same One I pray. Amen. *9/2/99*

Father, I pray that you will raise up women within your church, equipping and empowering them to be salt and light, teaching them to walk in the power of the Holy Spirit and to be busy about your kingdom work. *7/30/00*

Dear Father, my heart's desire is to accomplish those good works mentioned in Ephesians 2:10 during this season of my life. *1/01/01*

Dear Father, thank you for reminding me so clearly about my attitude toward leadership. I pray that what you taught in Hebrews 13:17 will be a reality in my life and in all women you call into leadership within your church—that we will obey our leaders and submit to their authority. Thank you for reminding us that leaders keep watch as men who must give account. May we obey them so their work will be a joy, not a burden. *7/13/01*

Dear Father, I read 2 Corinthians 3:4–6 as your directive for this new season in women's ministry. That we are not competent within ourselves to claim anything, but our competence comes from God. Therefore, since we have this ministry, may we not lose heart, for we do not preach ourselves in any way but Jesus Christ as Lord, and ourselves as your servants for his sake. *10/30/01*

Father, I pray you will release the constraints of the societal church and, in the meantime, set women's hearts free within the constraints. *1/02/03*

Father, I pray Ephesians 2:21–22 today for the women of our church, that in him we are all joined together and rise to become a holy temple in the Lord, being built together to become a dwelling in which God lives by his Spirit. *6/16/03*

Father, sometimes I still feel like Moses when he said, "I am only a little child and do not know how to carry out my duties . . . so give your servant a discerning heart to govern your people and to distinguish between right and wrong." *07/10/04*

Father, please give me the Spirit of wisdom and revelation so that I may know you better. *9/22/05*

APPENDIX 10

SAMPLE WOMEN'S MINISTRIES MISSION STATEMENTS

Use these sample mission statements as inspiration in writing your own:

To encourage spiritual growth in women through the study of God's Word, the cultivation of relationships, and the promotion of evangelistic outreach.

(a) To extend God's grace to broken and searching women. (b) To empower women for ministry and leadership. (c) To support and encourage women in their Christian walk and day-to-day life. (d) To provide opportunities for women to reach out to seeking friends.

To serve and minister to women inside and outside the church through teaching the Word of God, providing fellowship and evangelism with the purpose of equipping and encouraging a deeper walk with Jesus Christ.

(a) To provide opportunities for women to be involved in Bible study and fellowship with other women. (b) To equip women to minister in their arena of influence. (c) To equip women to serve others in the church through their spiritual gifts. (d) To develop ministries to women in the area of prayer and that meet specific needs. (e) To provide opportunities for outreach to women in the surrounding community.

To provide opportunities for all women of the church to grow toward maturity in Christ through worship, study, service, fellowship, and evangelism.

To facilitate women growing into mature followers of Christ by providing opportunities for spiritual growth and to equip women to serve God more effectively in their homes, their church, and their community.

To take the time to hear from, respond to, and seek God through prayer and worship, so that Christian women will be drawn closer to God and each other to study, understand, and apply his Word, as well as use their spiritual gifts in evangelism and other dimensions of kingdom work.

To encourage and equip women to follow Christ victoriously (Heb. 10:24–25).

APPENDIX 11

MINISTRY IN MOTION

Ministry in Motion is simply an email group of women who want to know about specific needs within the church and community. They understand that they are to be sensitive to the Holy Spirit's prompting to discern if he's asking them to respond to the need. Be sure to send the email to yourself and include the group recipients in a BCC (blind carbon copy), for privacy issues. The following sample of a Ministry in Motion email focuses on readability, effective communication of the need, and clarification of how to respond.

Sample #1:
To: (your email)
BCC: (group's emails)
Subject: Ministry in Motion

NEED: vacuum cleaner
A church member living on a minimum-wage salary needs to replace her vacuum cleaner. If you have one to donate,

let the women's office know by return email or by calling 000.000.0000. We'll ask you to drop it off at the WM's office at your earliest convenience!

Serving together,
Your name

Sample #2:
To: (you)
BCC: (group)
Subject: Ministry in Motion

NEED: Childcare for a two-year-old
A single mom attends class Tuesday and Thursday evenings for her GED. A government program supplements childcare expenses $6 per class. The classes last two hours, 6:00–8:00 p.m., and childcare costs run $15. Mom needs both someone to keep her daughter and assistance with additional expenses. Contact the women's office by return email or by calling 000.000.0000.

Serving together,
Your name

NOTES

Introduction

1. Weekly support group for single moms.
2. Christ-centered twelve-step recovery program, http://www.celebrate
recovery.com/index.shtml.

Chapter 1 Sisterhood: Those Who Came Before

1. Greek translation of Tabitha.
2. Modern-day Jaffa, a suburb of Tel Aviv, about thirty-eight miles from
Jerusalem on the Mediterranean.
3. Linda Lesniewski, *Drawn to the Cross* (Grand Rapids: Revell,
2005).

Chapter 2 Hearing God's Voice

1. See appendix 1 for the complete story.
2. Paramount Pictures, 1945.

Chapter 3 Making the Choice

1. Bruce Wilkinson, *The Dream Giver* (Sisters, OR: Multnomah, 2003),
93.
2. Michael Guido, http://www.guidogardens.com/.
3. Wilkinson, *Dream Giver*, 102.

Chapter 4 Me, a Leader?

1. Lesniewski, *Drawn to the Cross*.
2. Gene Wilkes, *Jesus on Leadership* (Nashville: LifeWay, 1996).

3. Thomas N. McGaffey, *The Courage to Lead* (Dallas: McGaffey, 1997).

4. http://lecturemanagement.com/speakers/ruby-payne.

5. Bob Briner with Lawrence Kimbrough, *Women in Leadership* (Nashville: Broadman, 1999).

6. Oswald Chambers, *My Utmost for His Highest* (Uhrichsville, OH: Barbour, 1993).

7. John Steinbeck, *East of Eden*, quoted in Jennifer Kennedy Dean, *The Life-Changing Power in the Name of Jesus* (Birmingham, AL: New Hope, 2004), 11.

8. http://www.coaching@kimberlychastain.com.

9. http://www.christa.net.

10. http://leadnet.org/.

11. CCN, Church Communication Network, http://www.ccnonline. net/.

12. Women's Ministry.NET; JR@jenniferrothschild.com.

Chapter 5 Launching or Expanding a Ministry

1. Wilkinson, *Dream Giver*, 77–78.

2. See appendix 3, Why Have a Women's Enrichment Ministry?

3. See appendix 3 for benefits of a women's ministry.

Chapter 7 Talking So Men Will Understand

1. John Gray, *Mars and Venus in the Workplace: A Practical Guide for Improving Communication and Getting Results at Work* (New York: HarperCollins, 2002).

2. Lysa TerKeurst, ed., *Leading Women to the Heart of God: Creating a Dynamic Women's Ministry* (Chicago: Moody, 2002), 102.

Chapter 9 Connecting through Women's Ministry

1. Patrick Butler, religion ed., "Ministry on the Road," *Tyler Morning News*, April 29, 2006, D1.

Chapter 10 Reaching Inward through Meeting Needs

1. http://www.barna.org/FlexPage.aspx?Page=BarnaUpdate& BarnaUpdateID=47.

2. Janet Thompson, *Woman to Woman Mentoring* (Nashville: LifeWay, 2000).

3. MOPS International, http://www.mops.org/.

4. Mom to Mom, http://www.momtomom.org/.

5. Mother Wise, http://www.motherwise.org/.

6. http://www.momsintouch.org/.

7. Fibromyalgia is a chronic syndrome characterized by muscle, joint or bone pain, and fatigue. Wikipedia.org.

8. Divorce Care, http://www.divorcecare.org/.

9. Online leader resources: http://www.lifeway.com/womenincrisis. A workbook example is H. Norman Wright with Learning Activities by Kay Moore, *Recovering from the Losses of Life*, Life Support Group Series Edition © 1995 by Fleming H. Revell (Nashville: LifeWay, 2005).

10. Brenda Branson and Paula Silva, "Domestic Violence Among Believers, Confronting the Destructive Secret," *Christian Counseling Today* 13, no. 3 (2005): 24.

11. Ibid., 25.

12. Marie M. Fortune, *Keeping the Faith: Guidance for Christian Women Facing Abuse* (San Francisco: HarperSanFrancisco, 1987).

13. Larry Crabb, *Connecting: Healing for Ourselves and Our Relationships* (Nashville: W Publishing Group, 1997), 43.

14. Ibid., 53.

15. Ibid., 127.

16. American Association of Christian Counselors, http://www.aacc.net, 1-800-526-8673.

17. Catherine Hart Weber, "Women and Depression," *Christian Counseling Today* 13, no. 4 (2005): 40–41. *Dysthimia*: A mood disorder characterized by chronic mildly depressed or irritable mood also called *dysthymic disorder*. Merriam-Webster Online Dictionary.

18. "Overcoming Depression" (Nashville: LifeWay, 1999).

19. *Friends*, NBC, 22 September 1994 through 6 May 2004.

20. Shannon Ethridge, *Every Woman's Battle: Discovering God's Plan for Sexual and Emotional Fulfillment* (Colorado Springs: WaterBrook, 2003).

21. Living Hope, Lasting Change, http://www.livehope.org.

22. Exodus International, http://www.exodus-international.org/.

23. Love Won Out conferences, http://lovewonout.com/.

24. Anne Paulk, *Restoring Sexual Identity* (Eugene, OR: Harvest House, 2003).

25. Ibid., 10.

26. More than 40 million Americans move each year. N.E.W. Ministries, Inc., http://www.justmoved.org, 1-866-587-8668.

27. See appendix 11 for a sample Ministry in Motion email.

Chapter 11 Nurturing Spiritual Growth

1. Shelley E. Taylor, *The Tending Instinct* (New York: Times Books, Holt and Co., 2002).

2. Lesniewski, *Drawn to the Cross*, 48.

3. The Praying Life Foundation, 1-888-844-6647; http://prayinglife.org/.

4. Jennifer Kennedy Dean, *Live a Praying Life: Open Your Life to God's Power and Provision* (Birmingham, AL: New Hope, 2003), 31.

5. Eugene Peterson, *Living the Resurrection: The Risen Christ in an Everyday Life* (Colorado Springs: NavPress, 2006), 35.

6. Angela Yee, *The Christian Conference Planner: Organizing Effective Events, Conferences, Retreats, Seminars, and Workshops* (Union City, CA: SummitStar Press, 2003).

7. The first woman to chair a department at the New Orleans Baptist Theological Seminary.

8. Sandy Denton has since written her story called *Splinters of Hope*. 281-395-2068, SandyD748@aol.com.

Chapter 12 Sustaining Freshness: For Yourself and Your Ministry

1. MOPS International. A support network of women sharing the bond of preschool children, http://www.mops.org/.

2. See http://www.womenary.com.

3. Fourth Partner Foundation, 909 ESE Loop 323, Suite 270, Tyler, TX 75701, 903-509-1771.

4. *World* magazine offers a window on the world with a Christian perspective. http://worldmag.com/index.cfm.

5. M. Rex Miller, *The Millennium Matrix* (San Francisco: Jossey-Bass, 2004), 139.

6. Ibid.

7. Ibid.

8. WomensMinistry.NET; JR@jenniferrothschild.com.

9. www.lifeway.com/women.

10. http://www.christianworkingwoman.org/. tcww@christianworkingwoman.org.

11. Over 300-plus ministries comprise Gospelcom.net Ministries located at http://www.gospelcom.net/ or http://www.christsites.com.

12. http://www.Crosswalk.com; or http://www.BibleGateway.com; or http://www.wikipedia.com for people, places, and things.

13. Richard A. Swenson, M.D., *The Overload Syndrome* (Colorado Springs: NavPress, 1998).

14. Tim Kimmel, *Little House on the Freeway* (Sisters, OR: Multnomah, 1994).

15. Lorry Lutz, *Women as Risk-Takers for God* (Grand Rapids: Baker, 1997), introduction.

16. Oswald Chambers, *My Utmost for His Highest* (Uhrichsville, OH: Barbour, 1993), 319.

Chapter 13 Leading Leaders

1. See the story of Esther in the book of Esther in the Old Testament.

2. Pamela Reeves, author, adviser, professor, and former dean of women at Multnomah Bible College and Seminary.

3. Beth Moore, Jill Briscoe, Sandra D. Wilson, *A Woman and Her God* (Brentwood, TN: Integrity, 2004), 40–41.

4. Women Reaching Women, www.lifeway.com/women.

5. Group Publishing Women's Leadership Conference, http://www.group.com/fillyourcup/.

6. Willowcreek Leadership Summit, http://www.willowcreek.com/conferences/index.asp.

7. Elmbrook Women's Events, http://www.elmbrook.org/events/women.asp.

8. Henry Cloud and John Townsend, *Boundaries* (Grand Rapids: Zondervan, 1992).

9. Stephen R. Graves and Thomas G. Addington, *The Fourth Frontier: Exploring the New World of Work* (Nashville: W Publishing Group, 2000).

Chapter 14 Developing Generational Leaders

1. Ken Hemphill, *Empowering Kingdom Growth* (Nashville: Broadman, 2004), 246.

2. BSF International, http://www.bsfinternational.org/Home/tabid/53/Default.aspx.

3. Jimmie Davis and Tep Lim, *Basic Needs of Today's Teen Girls*, Women's Ministry Planning Guide (2006), 2.

4. SAGE Ministries, http://www.sageministries.org/.

5. Yada Yada Events with Vicki Courtncy, http://www.vickicourtney.com/.

6. Lisa Bevere, http://www.messengerintl.org/.

7. George Barna, *Revolution* (Wheaton: Tyndale, 2005), 124–25.

Chapter 15 Reaching Outward through Meeting Needs

1. Diane Langberg, "Where to Now? Women as a Mission Field," *Christian Counseling Today* 13 (2005): 50, 51–53.

2. Ibid., 52–53.

3. "Methodist Churches Plan Mission Week Project," *Tyler Morning Telegraph*, June 15, 2006.

4. http://www.wmu.com/getinvolved/ministry/cwjc/.

5. The Magdalene Project, www.themagdaleneproject.org, info@themagdaleneproject.org, 512-292-1108.

Chapter 16 Sharing Your Faith

1. Jaye Martin, *Heartcall: Women Sharing God's Heart* (Alpharetta, GA: North American Mission Board of the Southern Baptist Convention, 1998). Jaye is the women's evangelism strategist in the Direct Evangelism Unit at the North American Mission Board. You can read her vision statement at http://www.namb.net/site/c.9qKILUOzEpH/b.238500/k.AB47/Jayes_Vision.html.

2. The National Day of Prayer occurs each year in May. http://www.ndptf.org/home/indexcfm?flash=1.

3. Campus Crusade for Christ International, http://www.evangelism.com/.

4. Women's Prayer Tea Brochures, http://imbresources.org/index.cfm/fa/store.prod/ProdID/1226.cfm.

5. Dan Allender, "What's Your Story?" Part I, *Christian Counseling Connection* 1 (2005): 12.

6. Miller, *Millennium*, 169.

7. Women Today Online, http://www.christianwomentoday.com; Journey of Joy, Box 300, Vancouver, B.C. V6C 2X3 Canada.

8. http://www.nooma.com/Shopping/NoomaStuff.aspx?cat=163&prod=311.

9. Salvation Army, http://www1.salvationarmy.org/ihq/www_sa.nsf.

10. Meals on Wheels, http://www.mealsonwheelsgreenville.org/about/about_mow.shtml.

11. Graves and Addington, *Fourth Frontier*.

12. American Tract Society, http://www.atstracts.org/readarticle.php?id=14.

13. www.digitracts.com.

14. *Outreach*, 2230 Oak Ridge Way, Vista, CA 92081-8341, 760-940-0600.

15. Marilyn Meberg, *The Decision of a Lifetime: The Most Important Choice You'll Ever Make* (Nashville: W Publishing Group, 2003).

16. Evangecube, http://www.evangecube.org/evangecube.html.

Chapter 17 Equipping and Sending

1. English Language Institute, http://www.elic.org/.

2. Rafiki Foundation, http://www.rafiki-foundation.org/rafiki_exchange.html.

3. World Crafts Catalogue, http://www.wmu.com/products/world crafts/.

4. David Forward, *The Essential Guide to the Short Term Mission Trip* (Chicago: Moody, 1998), 11.

5. Randy Sprinkle, *Follow Me: Lessons for Becoming a Prayerwalker* (Birmingham, AL: New Hope, 2001).

6. Steve Hawthorne and Graham Kendrick, *Prayerwalking: Praying On-Site with Insight* (Lake Mary, FL: Charisma House, 1993), quoted in ibid., 3–4. Randy Sprinkle states this phrase was first used by Steve Hawthorne.

7. Ibid., 5.

8. John F. Walvoord, Roy B. Zuck, eds., *The Bible Knowledge Commentary: An Exposition of the Scriptures* (Wheaton: Victor, 1983–1985).

Chapter 18 Contagious Devotion

1. Jennifer Kennedy Dean, *Legacy of Prayer, A Spiritual Trust Fund for the Generations* (Birmingham, AL: New Hope, 2002), 15. Moms in Touch encourages women to pray for their children. http://www.momsintouch.org/.

2. Mohr, "Find Us Faithful." © Birdwing Music/Jonathan Mark Music. All rights reserved. Used by permission.

BIBLIOGRAPHY

Adams, Chris, comp. *Transformed Lives: Taking Women's Ministry to the Next Level*. Nashville: LifeWay, 1999.

———. *Women Reaching Women: Beginning and Building a Growing Women's Ministry*. Nashville: LifeWay, 2005.

Barna, George. *State of the Church: 2005*. The Barna Group, 2005.

Blackaby, Henry, and Roy T. Edgemon. *The Ways of God*. Nashville: LifeWay, 2001.

Briner, Bob, and Lawrence Kimbrough. *Women in Leadership*. Nashville: Broadman, 1999.

Briscoe, Jill, Laurie Katz McIntyre, and Beth Seversen. *Designing Effective Women's Ministries, Choosing, Planning and Implementing the Right Programs for Your Church*. Grand Rapids: Zondervan, 1995.

Chambers, Oswald. *My Utmost for His Highest*. Uhrichsville, OH: Barbour, 1993.

Clark, Linda, comp. *Five Leadership Essentials for Women*. Birmingham, AL: New Hope, 2004.

Crabb, Larry. *Connecting: Healing for Ourselves and Our Relationships*. Nashville: W Publishing Group, 1997.

Dean, Jennifer Kennedy. *The Life-Changing Power in the Name of Jesus*. Birmingham, AL: New Hope, 2004.

————. *Live a Praying Life*. Birmingham, AL: New Hope, 2003.

Duncan, Ligon, and Susan Hunt. *Women's Ministry in the Local Church*. Wheaton: Crossway, 2006.

Ethridge, Shannon. Introduction by Stephen Arterburn. *Every Woman's Battle*. Colorado Springs: WaterBrook, 2003.

Finzel, Hans. *The Top Ten Mistakes Leaders Make*. Wheaton: Victor, 1994.

Fortune, Marie M. *Keeping the Faith: Guidance for Christian Women Facing Abuse*. San Francisco: Harper, 1987.

Forward, David. *The Essential Guide to the Short Term Mission Trip*. Chicago: Moody, 1998.

Graves, Stephen R., and Thomas G. Addington. *The Fourth Frontier: Exploring the New World of Work*. Nashville: W Publishing Group, 2000.

Gray, John. *Mars and Venus in the Workplace: A Practical Guide for Improving Communication and Getting Results at Work*. New York: HarperCollins, 2001.

Hemphill, Ken. *Empowering Kingdom Growth*. Nashville: Broadman, 2004.

————. *Serving God: Discovering and Using Your Spiritual Gifts*. Dallas: Sampson Co., 1995.

Kelly, Rhonda. *A Woman's Guide to Servant Leadership: A Biblical Study for Becoming a Christlike Leader*. Birmingham, AL: New Hope, 2002.

Kent, Carol. *Becoming a Woman of Influence*. Colorado Springs: NavPress, 1999.

Kimball, Dan. *The Emerging Church*. Grand Rapids: Zondervan, 2003.

Kimmel, Tim. *Little House on the Freeway*. Sisters, OR: Multnomah, 1994.

Malphurs, Aubrey. *Being Leaders: The Nature of Authentic Christian Leadership*. Grand Rapids: Baker, 2003.

Miller, Rex. *The Millennium Matrix*. San Fransisco: Jossey-Bass, 2004.

Myers, Ruth, with Warren Myers. *31 Days of Praise*. Sisters, OR: Multnomah, 1994.

Parrott III, Les. *High-Maintenance Relationships: How to Handle Impossible People*. Wheaton: Tyndale, 1996.

Paulk, Anne. *Restoring Sexual Identity*. Eugene, OR: Harvest House, 2003.

Peterson, Eugene. *Living the Resurrection: The Risen Christ in Everyday Life*. Colorado Springs: NavPress, 2006.

Porter, Carol, and Mike Hamel, eds. *Women's Ministry Handbook*. Colorado Springs: Victor, 1992.

Rogers, Debi, and Mike Rogers. *The Kingdom Agenda: Experiencing God in Your Workplace*. Nashville: LifeWay, 1997.

Sprinkle, Randy. *Follow Me: Lessons for Becoming a Prayerwalker*. Birmingham, AL: New Hope, 2001.

Swenson, Richard. *The Overload Syndrome*. Colorado Springs: NavPress, 1998.

Taylor, Shelley. *The Tending Instinct*. New York: Times Book, Holt and Company, 2002.

TerKeurst, Lysa, ed. *Leading Women to the Heart of God: Creating a Dynamic Women's Ministry*. Chicago: Moody, 2002.

Thompson, Janet. *Woman to Woman Mentoring*. Nashville: LifeWay, 2000.

Walvoord, John F., and Roy B. Zuck, eds. *The Bible Knowledge Commentary. An Exposition of the Scriptures*. Wheaton: Victor, 1983–1985.

Waterman, Linda McGinn. *Resource Guide for Women's Ministry*. Nashville: Broadman, 2005.

Linda Lesniewski serves as the women's ministry coordinator at Green Acres Baptist Church in Tyler, Texas. A trainer for LifeWay Christian resources and a frequent speaker at women's leadership conferences and training seminars, Linda is author of *Women at the Cross* and a contributing author for *Transformed Lives: Taking Women's Ministry to the Next Level*. She and her husband of thirty-five years live in Tyler, Texas. They have four young adult children and two granddaughters.